# ΑΙΣΧΥΛΟΥ
## Ευμενίδες

# AESCHYLUS'
## *Eumenides*

A Dual Language Edition

*Greek Text Edited (1926) by*
Herbert Weir Smyth

*English Translation and Notes by*
Ian Johnston

*Edited by*
Evan Hayes and Stephen Nimis

FAENUM PUBLISHING
OXFORD, OHIO

*Aeschylus* Eumenides: *A Dual Language Edition*
First Edition

© 2017 by Faenum Publishing

All rights reserved. Subject to the exception immediately following, this book may not be reproduced, in whole or in part, in any form (beyond copying permitted by Sections 107 and 108 of the U.S. Copyright Law and except by reviewers for the public press), without written permission from the publisher.

A version of this work has been made available under a Creative Commons Attribution-Noncommercial-Share Alike 3.0 License. The terms of the license can be accessed at creativecommons.org.

Accordingly, you are free to copy, alter and distribute this work under the following conditions:

You must attribute the work to the author (but not in a way that suggests that the author endorses your alterations to the work).
You may not use this work for commercial purposes.
If you alter, transform or build up this work, you may distribute the resulting work only under the same or similar license as this one.

ISBN-10: 1940997860
ISBN-13: 9781940997865

Published by Faenum Publishing, Ltd.
Cover Design: Evan Hayes

for Geoffrey (1974-1997)

οἵη περ φύλλων γενεὴ τοίη δὲ καὶ ἀνδρῶν.
φύλλα τὰ μέν τ᾽ ἄνεμος χαμάδις χέει, ἄλλα δέ θ᾽ ὕλη
τηλεθόωσα φύει, ἔαρος δ᾽ ἐπιγίγνεται ὥρη:
ὣς ἀνδρῶν γενεὴ ἣ μὲν φύει ἣ δ᾽ ἀπολήγει.

Generations of men are like the leaves.
In winter, winds blow them down to earth,
but then, when spring season comes again,
the budding wood grows more. And so with men:
one generation grows, another dies away. (*Iliad* 6)

# TABLE OF CONTENTS

# EDITORS' NOTE

This book presents the Greek text of Aeschylus' *Eumenides* with a facing English translation. The Greek text is that of Herbert Weir Smyth (1926), which is in the public domain and available as a pdf. This text has also been digitized by the Perseus Project (perseus.tufts.edu). The English translation and accompanying notes are those of Ian Johnston of Vancouver Island University, Nanaimo, BC. This translation is available freely on-line (records.viu.ca/~johnstoi/). We have reset both texts, making a number of very minor corrections, and placed them on opposing pages. This facing-page format will be useful to those wishing to read the English translation while looking at the Greek version, or vice versa.

# Lecture on the *Oresteia*

## by Ian Johnston

*The following notes began as a lecture delivered, in part, at Malaspina College (now Vancouver Island University) in Liberal Studies 301 on September 25, 1995. That lecture was considerably revised in July 2000. This text is in the public domain, released July 2000. Note that references to Aeschylus's text are to the translation by Robert Fagles (Penguin, 1977).*

## Introduction

My lecture today falls into two parts. In the first I want to offer some background information for our study of Aeschylus's *Oresteia*, specifically on the Trojan War and the House of Atreus, and in the second I will be addressing the first play in that trilogy, the *Agamemnon*, making relatively brief mention of the other plays in the trilogy. Other speakers today will focus in more detail on the second and third plays.

## The Trojan War

With the possible exception of the narratives in the Old Testament, no story has been such a fecund artistic resource in Western culture as the Greeks' favourite tale, the Trojan War. This is a vast, complex story, which includes a great many subsidiary narratives, and it has over the centuries proved an inexhaustible resource for Western writers, painters, musicians, choreographers, novelists, and dramatists. It would be comparatively easy and very interesting to develop a course of study of Western Culture based entirely upon artistic depictions of events from this long narrative. So it's an important part of cultural literacy for any students of our traditions to have some acquaintance with the details of this story, which even today shows no sign of losing its appeal.

There is not time here today to go into the narrative in any depth. So I'm going to be dealing only with a very brief treatment of those details most immediately pertinent to our study of Aeschylus. However, for those who want to go over a more comprehensive summary of the total narrative, see p. xxiii.

The complete narrative of the Trojan War includes at least six sections: the long-term causes (the Judgment of Paris), the immediate causes (the seduction of Helen of Troy by Paris), the preparations (especially the gathering of the forces at Aulis and the sacrifice of Iphigeneia), the events of the war (climaxing in the Wooden Horse and the destruction of the city), the returns (most notably the adventures of Odysseus and Aeneas and the murder of Agamemnon), and the long-term aftermath.

The total narrative is found by putting together many different versions, not all of which by any means agree on the details. Unlike the Old Testament narrative which was eventually codified into an official single version (at least for Christians and Jews), the story of the Trojan War exists in many versions of separate incidents in many different documents. There is no single authoritative account. Homer's *Iliad* and *Odyssey* enjoyed a unique authority in classical Greece, but those works deal only with a relatively small parts of the total narrative and are by no means the only texts which deal with the subject matter they cover.

Was the Trojan War a historical event or an endlessly embroidered fiction? The answer to this question is much disputed. The ancient Greeks believed in the historical truth of the tale and dated it at approximately 1200 BC, about the same time as the Exodus of the Israelites from Egypt. Until the last century, however, most later Europeans thought of the story as a poetic invention. This attitude changed quickly when a rich German merchant, Schliemann, in the nineteenth century, explored possible sites for the city (using Homeric geography as a clue) and unearthed some archeological remains of a city, one version of which had apparently been violently destroyed at about the traditional date. The site of this city, in Hissarlik in modern Turkey, is now widely believed to be the historical site of ancient Troy (although we cannot be certain).

What we need to know as background for Aeschylus's play is a comparatively small portion of this total narrative, which Aeschylus assumes his audience will be thoroughly familiar with. The expedition against Troy was initiated as a response to the seduction of Helen by Paris, a son of Priam, King of Troy, and their running off together back to Troy with a great quantity of Spartan treasure. Helen, the daughter of Zeus and Leda, was married to Menelaus, king of Sparta. His brother, Agamemnon, was king of Argos, married to Helen's twin sister Clytaemnestra (but whose father was not Zeus).

As a result of the abduction of Helen, the Greeks mounted an expedition against Troy, headed up by the two kings, Agamemnon and Menelaus, the sons of Atreus, or the Atreidai. They summoned their allies to meet them with troops at Aulis, where the ships were to take the troops on board and sail to Troy.

However, Agamemnon had angered the goddess Artemis by killing a sacred animal. So Artemis sent contrary winds, and the fleet could not sail. The entire expedition was threatened with failure. Finally, the prophet Calchas informed the Greek leadership that the fleet would not be able to sail unless

Agamemnon sacrificed his eldest daughter, Iphigeneia. He did so, and the fleet sailed to Troy, where, after ten years of siege, the city finally fell to the Greeks, who then proceeded to rape, pillage, and destroy the temples of the Trojans. The Greek leaders divided up the captive women. Agamemnon took Cassandra, a daughter of king Priam, home as a slave concubine. Cassandra had refused the sexual advances of the god Apollo; he had punished her by giving her the gift of divine prophecy but making sure that no one ever believed her.

The moral construction put on the Trojan War varies a good deal from one writer to the next. Homer's *Iliad*, for example, sees warfare as a condition of existence and therefore the Trojan War is a symbol for life itself, a life in which the highest virtues are manifested in a tragic heroism. In the *Odyssey*, there is a strong sense that the warrior life Odysseus has lived at Troy is something he must learn to abandon in favour of something more suited to home and hearth. Euripides used the stories of the war to enforce either a very strong anti-war vision or to promote highly unnaturalistic and ironic romance narratives.

In Aeschylus's play there is a strong sense that the Trojan War is, among other things, an appropriate act of revenge for the crime of Paris and Helen against Menelaus. And yet, at the same time, it is something which most of the people at home despise, for it kills all the young citizens and corrupts political life by taking the leaders away. In fact, the complex contradictions in the Chorus's attitude to that war help to bring out one of the major points of the first play: the problematic nature of justice based on a simple revenge ethic. According to the traditional conception of justice, Agamemnon is right to fight against Troy; but the effort is destroying his own city. So how can that be right?

## The House of Atreus

The other background story which Aeschylus assumes his audience will be thoroughly familiar with is the story of the House of Atreus. This story, too, is recounted in more detail in the note on the Trojan War mentioned above.

The important point to know for the play is that the House of Atreus suffers from an ancient curse. As part of the working out of this curse, Agamemnon's father, Atreus, had quarreled violently with his brother Thyestes. As a result of this quarrel, Atreus had killed Thyestes's sons and fed them to him at a reconciliation banquet. In some versions of the story, Thyestes, overcome with horror, produced a child with his surviving daughter in order to have someone to avenge the crime. The offspring of that sexual union was Aegisthus (Aeschylus changes this point by having Aegisthus an infant at the time of the banquet). Aegisthus' actions in the *Oresteia*, the seduction of Clytaemnestra (before the play starts) and the killing of Agamemnon, he interprets and excuses as a revenge for what Atreus did to his father and brothers. (For a more detailed summary account of the story of the House of Atreus, see p. xxxv.)

The House of Atreus is probably the most famous secular family in our literary history, partly because it tells the story of an enormous family curse, full of sex, violence, horrible deaths going on for generations. It also throws into relief a theme which lies at the very centre of the *Oresteia* and which has intrigued our culture ever since, the nature of revenge.

## *The Revenge Ethic*

Aechylus's trilogy, and especially the first play, calls our attention repeatedly to a central concept of justice: justice as revenge. This is a relatively simple notion, and it has a powerful emotional appeal, even today. The revenge ethic, simply put, makes justice the personal responsibility of the person insulted or hurt or, if that person is dead, of someone closely related to him, almost invariably a close blood relative. The killer must be killed, and that killing must be carried out personally by the most appropriate person, who accepts that charge as an obvious responsibility. It is a radically simple and powerfully emotional basis for justice, linking retribution to the family and their feelings for each other and for their collective honour.

We have already met this ethic in the Old Testament and in the *Odyssey*. In the latter book, the killing of Aegisthus by Orestes is repeatedly referred to with respect and approval: it was a just act because Aegisthus had violated Orestes's home and killed his father. And we are encouraged to see Odysseus's extraordinarily violent treatment of the suitors and their followers as a suitable revenge, as justice, for what they have done or tried to do to his household, especially his goods, his wife, and his son. Justice demands a personal, violent, and effective response from an appropriate family member.

And we are very familiar with this ethic from our own times, because justice as revenge seems to be an eternally popular theme of movies, televisions, books. It has become an integral part of the Western movie and of the police drama. Some actors create a career out of the genre (e.g., Charles Bronson and Arnold Swartzenegger and the Godfather).

We may not ourselves base our justice system directly and simply upon revenge, but we all understand very clearly those feelings which prompt a desire for revenge (especially when we think of any violence done to members of our own family), and we are often very sympathetic to those who do decide to act on their own behalf in meting out justice to someone who has killed someone near and dear to them.

So in reading the *Oresteia* we may be quite puzzled by the rather strange way the story is delivered to us, but there is no mistaking the importance or the familiarity of the issue. One way of approaching this play, in fact, is to see it primarily as an exploration of the adequacy of the revenge ethic as a proper basis for justice in the community and the movement towards a more civilized, effective, and rational way of judging crimes in the polis.

## An Important Preliminary Interlude

Before going on to make some specific remarks about the *Agamemnon*, I'd like to call attention to an interpretative problem that frequently (too frequently) crops up with the *Oresteia*, especially among students, namely, the desire to treat this work as if it were, first and foremost, a philosophical investigation into concepts of justice rather than a great artistic fiction, a poetic exploration.

Why is this important? Well, briefly put, treating the play as if it were a rational argument on the order of, say, a Socratic enquiry, removes from our study of it the most important poetic qualities of the work. We concentrate all our discussions on the conceptual dimensions of the play, attending to the logic of Agamemnon's defense of his actions, or Clytaemnestra's of hers, or the final verdict of Athena in the trial of Orestes at the end, and we strive, above all, to evaluate the play on the basis of our response to the rational arguments put forward.

This approach is disastrous because the *Oresteia* is not a rational argument. It is, by contrast, an artistic exploration of conceptual issues. What matters here are the complex states of feeling which emerge from the characters, the imagery, the actions, and the ideas (as they are expressed by particular characters in the action). What we are dealing with here, in other words, is much more a case of how human beings feel about justice, about the possibilities for realizing justice in the fullest sense of the word within the human community, than a rational blueprint for implementing a new system.

I'll have more to say about this later, but let me give just one famous example. The conclusion of the trilogy will almost certainly create problems for the interpreter who seeks, above all else, a clearly worked out rational system for achieving justice in the community (understanding the rational justification for Athena's decision in the trial or the reconciliation with the Furies, for example, will be difficult to work out precisely). But Aeschylus, as a poet, is not trying to offer such a conclusion. What he gives us is a symbolic expression of our highest hopes, our most passionate desires for justice (which is so much more than a simple objective concept). The ending of the trilogy, with all those people (who earlier were bitter opponents) on stage singing and dancing in harmony, is a celebration of human possibility (and perhaps a delicate one at that), not the endorsement of a clearly codified system.

In the same way Athena's decision to acquit Orestes is not primarily the expression of a reasoned argument. It is far more an artistic symbol evocative of our highest hopes. This point needs to be stressed because (for understandable reasons) this part of the play often invites a strong feminist critique, as if what is happening here is the express desire to suppress feminine power. Now, I would be the last to deny the importance of the gendered imagery in the trilogy, but here I would also insist that Athena is a goddess, and her actions are, in effect, endorsing a shift in power from the divine to the human. Justice will no longer be a helpless appeal to the justice of Zeus in an endless sequence of killings: it will be the highest responsibility of the human community. The play does not "prove" that that's a good idea. It celebrates that as a possibility (and it may well be significant that that important hope is realized on stage by a divine power who is *female* but who is not caught up in the powerful nexus of the traditional family, since she sprung fully grown from Zeus' head).

This does not mean, I hasten to add, that we should abandon our reason as we approach the play. It does mean, however, that we must remain alert to the plays in the trilogy as works of art, and especially as dramatic works, designed to communicate their insights to us in performance. Yes, the plays deal with ideas, and we need to come to terms with those. But these ideas are never separate from human desires, motives, and passions. To see what Aeschylus is doing here, then, we need to look very carefully at all the various ways in which this emotional dimension, the full range of ambiguity and irony, establishes itself in the imagery, metaphors, and actions. We need, for example, always to be aware of how the way characters express their thoughts (especially the images they use) qualifies, complicates, and often undercuts the most obvious meanings of their words.

You will get a firm sense of what I mean if you consider that no one would ever put the *Oresteia* on a reading list for a philosophy course (except perhaps as background). Yet the work obviously belongs on any list of the world's great poetic dramas. We need to bear that in mind in our discussions, basing what we say on close readings of the text rather than on easy generalizations imposed on complex ironies.

## Revenge in the Agamemnon

In the *Agamemnon*, revenge is the central issue. Agamemnon interprets his treatment of Troy as revenge for the crime of Paris and Helen; Clytaemnestra interprets her killing of Agamemnon as revenge for the sacrifice of Iphigeneia; Aegisthus interprets his role in the killing of Agamemnon as revenge for the treatment of his half-brothers by Agamemnon's father, Atreus. We are constantly confronted in this play with the realities of what revenge requires and what it causes, and we are always being asked to evaluate the justification for killing by appeals to the traditional revenge ethic.

But there's more to it than that. For in this play, unlike the *Odyssey*, revenge emerges as something problematic, something that, rather than upholding and restoring the polis, is threatening to engulf it in an unending cycle of destruction, until the most powerful city in the Greek world is full of corpses and vultures. In fact, one of the principal purposes of the first play of the trilogy is to force us to recognize that justice based on revenge creates special difficulties which it cannot solve. To use one of the most important images in the play, the city is caught in a net from which there seems to be no escape. The traditional revenge ethic has woven a cycle of necessary destruction around the city, and those caught in the mesh feel trapped in a situation they do not want but cannot alter.

## The Chorus in the Agamemnon

The major way in which Aeschylus presents revenge to us as a problem in the *Agamemnon* is through the actions and the feelings of the Chorus. For us the huge part given to the Chorus is unfamiliar, and we may be tempted from time to time to skip a few pages until the next person enters, and the action moves forward. That is a major mistake, because following what is happening to the Chorus in the *Agamemnon* is essential to understanding the significance of what is going on. They provide all sorts of necessary background information, but, more important than that, they set the emotional and moral tone of the city. What they are, what they say, and how they feel represent the quality of life (in the full meaning of that term) available in the city.

First of all, who are these people? They are adult male citizens of Argos, those who ten years ago were too old to join the expedition to Troy. Hence, they are extremely old and very conscious of their own physical feebleness. And they are worried. They know the history of this family; they know very well about the sacrifice of Iphigeneia; and they have a very strong sense of what Clytaemnestra is about to do. They are full of an ominous sense of what is in store, and yet they have no means of dealing with that or even talking about it openly. Thus, in everything they say until quite near the end of the play, there is a very strong feeling of moral evasiveness: Agamemnon is coming home, and justice awaits. They know what that means. It is impossible to read very much of those long choruses without deriving a firm sense of their unease at what is going to happen and of their refusal and inability to confront directly the sources of that unease.

Why should this create problems for them? Well, they are caught in something of a dilemma. On the one hand, the only concept of justice they understand is the traditional revenge ethic: the killer must be killed. At the same time, they are weary of the slaughter. They are fearful for the future of their city, since the revenge ethic is destroying its political fabric. And they don't approve of what Clytaemnestra and Aegisthus are up to. They may sense that there's a certain "justice" in the revenge for Iphigeneia, but they are not satisfied that that is how things should be done, because Agamemnon, or someone like him, is necessary for the survival of the city.

In that sense their long account of the sacrifice of Iphigeneia is much more than simply narrative background. They are probing the past, searching through the sequence of events, as if somehow the justice of what has happened will emerge if they focus on the history which has led up to this point. But the effort gets them nowhere, and they are left with the desperately weak formulaic cry, "Let all go well," a repetitive prayer expressing a slim hope for a better future. They don't like what's happened in the past, but they cannot come to a mature acceptance of it, because it scares them. The actions of Agamemnon seem to fit the concept of justice, as they understand the term, but the actions themselves are horrific. They want it to make sense, but they cannot themselves derive any emotional satisfaction from the story or from what they suspect will happen next.

Thus, everything they utter up to the murder of Agamemnon is filled with a sense of moral unease and emotional confusion. They want the apparently endless cycle of retributive killings to stop, but they have no way of conceptualizing or imagining how that might happen. Their historical circumstances are too emotionally complex for the system of belief they have at hand to interpret the significance of those events. Since the only system of justice they have ever known tells them that the killings must continue and since they don't want them to continue, they are paralyzed. The physical weakness throughout much of the play is an obvious symbol for their moral and emotional paralysis. In fact, the most obvious thing about Argos throughout this first play is the moral duplicity and evasiveness of everyone in it.

This moral ambiguity of Argos manifests itself repeatedly in the way the Chorus and others refuse to reveal publicly what they are thinking and feeling. Right from the very opening of the play, in the Watchman's speech, what is for a brief moment an outburst of spontaneous joy at the news that Agamemnon will be returning is snuffed out with a prudent hesitancy and an admission that in Argos one does not dare utter one's thoughts. "I could tell you things if I wanted to," admits the Watchman, "but in this city an ox stands on my tongue."

The way in which the watchman's joy is instantly tempered by his guarded suspicion indicates, right at the very opening of the play, that we are in a murky realm here, where people are not free to state what they feel, where one feeling cancels out another, and where there's no sense of what anyone might do to resolve an unhappy situation.

It's important to note here that the political inertia of the old men of the chorus is not a function of their cowardice or their stupidity. They are neither of these. It comes from a genuine sense of moral and emotional confusion. As mentioned above, in order to understand their situation they are constantly reviewing the past, bringing to our attention the nature of the warfare in Troy (which they hate), the terrible destruction caused by Helen (whom they despise), the awful sacrifice of Iphigeneia (for whom they express great sympathy), and so on. The moral code they have inherited tells them that, in some way or another, all these things are just. But that violates their feelings. Revenge, they realize, is not achieving what justice in the community is supposed, above all else, to foster, a secure and fair life in the polis, an emotional satisfaction with our communal life together. On the contrary, it is destroying Argos and will continue to do so, filling its citizens with fear and anxiety.

This attitude reaches its highest intensity in the interview they have with Cassandra. She unequivocally confronts them with their deepest fears: that they will see Agamemnon dead. Their willed refusal to admit that they understand what she is talking about is not a sign of their stupidity--they know very well what she means. But they cannot admit that to themselves, because then they would have to do something about it, and they have no idea what they should or could do. If they do nothing, then perhaps the problem will go away. Maybe Agamemnon can take care of it. Or, put another way, before acting decisively, they need a reason to act. But the traditional reasons behind justice are telling them that they have no right to intervene.

The situation does not go away of course. Agamemnon is killed, and Clytaemnestra emerges to deliver a series of triumphant speeches over his corpse. It is particularly significant to observe what happens to the Chorus of old men at this point. They have no principled response to Clytaemnestra, but they finally are forced to realize that what has just happened is, in some fundamental way, a violation of what justice in the polis should be all about, and that they therefore should not accept it. And this emotional response rouses them to action: for the first time they openly defy the rulers of the city, at some risk to themselves. They have no carefully worked out political agenda, nor can they conceptualize what they are doing. Their response is radically emotional: the killing of the king must be wrong. Civil war is averted, because Clytaemnestra and Aegisthus do not take up the challenge, retiring to the palace. But the end of the *Agamemnon* leaves us with the most graphic image of a city divided against itself. What has gone on in the name of justice is leading to the worst of all possible communal disasters, civil war, the most alarming manifestation of the total breakdown of justice.

This ending is, in part, not unlike the ending of the *Odyssey*, where Odysseus's revenge against the suitors initiates a civil war between him and his followers and those whose duty it is to avenge the slain. But Homer does not pursue the potential problem of justice which this poses. Instead he wraps the story up quickly with a divine intervention, which forcibly imposes peace on the antagonists. We are thus not invited to question the justice of Odysseus's actions, which in any case have divine endorsement throughout.

In Aeschylus's first play, by contrast, the problems of a city divided against itself by the inadequacy of the revenge ethic become the major focus of the second and third plays, which seek to find a way through the impasse.

## Agamemnon and Clytaemnestra

In contrast to the moral difficulties of the Chorus, the two main characters in the *Agamemnon*, Agamemnon and Clytaemnestra, have no doubts about what justice involves: it is based upon revenge. And the two of them act decisively in accordance with the old ethic to destroy those whom the code decrees must be destroyed, those whom they have a personal responsibility to hurt in the name of vengeance for someone close to them.

Now, in accordance with that old revenge code, both of them have a certain justification for their actions (which they are not slow to offer). But Aeschylus's treatment of the two brings out a very important limitation of the revenge ethic, namely the way in which it is compromised by the motivation of those carrying out justice.

For in spite of their enmity for each other, Agamemnon and Clytaemnestra have some obvious similarities. They live life to satisfy their own immediate desires for glory and power, and to gratify their immoderate passions, particularly their blood lust. Whatever concerns they have for the polis take second place to the demands of their own passionate natures. They do not suffer the same moral anguish as the Chorus because they feel powerful enough to act on how they feel and because their very strong emotions about themselves are not in the slightest tempered by a sense of what is best for the city or for anyone else. Their enormously powerful egos insist that they don't have to attend to anyone else's opinion (the frequency of the personal pronouns "I," "me," "mine," and "my" in their speech is really significant). They answer only to themselves.

More than this, the way in which each of the two main characters justifies the bloody revenge carried out in the name of justice reveals very clearly that they revel in blood killing. Shedding blood with a maximum of personal savagery, without any limit, gratifies each of them intensely, so much so that their joy in destruction calls into question their veracity in talking of themselves as agents of justice.

This is so pronounced a feature of these heroic figures that the play puts a certain amount of pressure on us to explore their motivation. They both claim they act in order to carry out justice. But do they? What other motives have come into play? When Agamemnon talks of how he obliterated Troy or walks on the red carpet or Clytaemnestra talks with delight about what a sexual charge she is going to get by making love to Aegisthus on top of the dead body of Agamemnon, we are surely invited to see that, however much they justify their actions with appeals to divine justice, their motivation has become very muddied with other, less noble motives.

Such observations may well occasion some dispute among interpreters. But in order to address them we need to pay the closest possible attention to the language and the motivation of these characters (as that is revealed in the language), being very careful not to accept too quickly the justifications they offer for their own actions. We need to ask ourselves repeatedly: On the basis of the language, how am I to understand the reasons why Agamemnon killed Iphigeneia and wiped out Troy? Why does Clytaemnestra so enjoy killing Agamemnon? If a disinterested sense of justice is all that is in play here, they why does she so enjoy killing Cassandra? Why, for that matter, does Agamemnon talk about the total destruction of Troy with such grim pleasure? Why does he get so much joy in talking about how he is going to bring justice back to Argos with a sword?

And this, I take it, is for Aeschylus a very important limitation on the revenge ethic. It brings into play concerns which have, on the face of it, no immediate connections with justice and everything to do with much baser human instincts. People like Agamemnon and Clytaemnestra, who claim (after the fact) to kill in the name of justice, actually are carrying out the destruction to satisfy much deeper, more urgent, and far less worthy human urges (a fact which may account for the fact that in their killing they go to excess, well beyond the strict demands of justice).

For that reason, Aeschylus gives us a very close look at the characters of Clytaemnestra and Agamemnon. As I say, we need to pay the closest attention to their language, trying to get a handle, not just on the surface details of what they are saying, but on the emotional complexities of the character uttering the lines. We need to ask ourselves the key question: In acting the way they do and for the reasons they state or reveal to us in their language, are they being just? Or is their sense of justice merely a patina covering something else? Or are both possibilities involved?

For instance, Clytaemnestra states that she killed Agamemnon in order to avenge Iphigeneia. Is that true? If it is a reason, how important is it? What else is involved here? In the second play, she confronts Orestes with this justification. But what is our response right at the moment after she has just done the deed? One needs here not merely to look at what she says but at how she says it. What particular emotions is she revealing in her style of speech and what do these reveal about her motives?

xix

Such questions become all the more important when we compare how they set about their acts of "justice" with the opening of the second play, when we see Orestes return to carry out the next chapter in the narrative of the House of Atreus. For there's a really marked difference between his conduct and that of his parents. A great deal of the second play is taken up with Orestes' preparations to carry out his vision of justice. It's not unimportant that much of that time he's questioning himself, seeking advice from others, involving others publicly in what he feels he has to do. In a sense, he is trying to purge himself of those emotions which drive Agamemnon and Clytaemnestra to their acts of "justice," to make himself an agent of divine justice rather than serving his own blood-lust.

This, I take it, is a key element in Aeschylus's treatment of the theme of justice. So long as the revenge ethic rests in the hands of people like Agamemnon and Clytaemnestra, tragically passionate egotists who answer only to their own immediate desires, the cycle of killing will go on for ever, and cities will destroy themselves in the blood feud. The only way out (and it is a hope) is that someone like Orestes will act out of a love of justice as a divine principle, setting aside as best he can (or even acting against) his deepest, most irrational blood feelings, thus moving beyond the revenge ethic.

We will get little sense of why Orestes deserves to be declared innocent unless we attend very carefully to the difference between his motives and those of his parents, for it is surely an important element in Athena's final judgment that the traditional revenge ethic, as embodied in the Furies and manifested in the conduct of Agamemnon, Clytaemnestra, and Aegisthus, is no longer compatible with justice in the community and that Orestes' actions in killing his mother are, as much as he can make them, undertaken in the service of others (Apollo and the community), rather than stemming from a passionate blood-lust (the fact that Orestes is willing to stand trial and abide by the verdict is one important sign of the difference between him and his parents).

## A Final Postscript

Human beings think about justice as a rational concept, institutionalized in their communities, but they also have strong emotions about justice, both within the family and the community. The revenge ethic harnessed to those powerful feelings in Aechylus's play stands exposed as something that finally violates our deepest sense of any possibility for enduring justice in our community, for it commits us a never-ending cycle of retributive killing and over-killing.

The *Oresteia* ends with a profound and very emotionally charged hope that the community can move beyond such a personally powerful emotional basis for justice and, with the sanction of the divine forces of the world, establish a system based on group discussion, consensus, juries (through what Athena calls persuasion)--in a word, can unite a conceptual, reasonable understanding of justice with our most powerful feelings about it. This work is, as Swinburne observed, one of the most optimistic visions of human life ever written, for it celebrates a dream we have that human beings in their communities can rule themselves justly, without recourse to blood vengeance, satisfying mind and heart in the process.

At the same time, however, Aeschylus is no shallow liberal thinker telling us to move beyond our brutal and unworkable traditions. For he understands that we cannot by some sleight of hand remove the Furies from our lives. They are ancient goddesses, eternally present. Hence, in the conclusion of the play the Furies, traditional goddesses of vengeance, are incorporated into the justice system, not excluded. And the powers they are given are significant: no city can thrive without them. Symbolically, the inclusion of the Furies in the final celebration, their new name (meaning "The Kindly Ones"), and their agreement fuse in a great theatrical display elements which were in open conflict only a few moments before.

It's as if the final image of this play stresses for us that in our justice we must strive to move beyond merely personal emotion (the basis of personal revenge) towards some group deliberations, but in the new process we must not violate our personal feelings or forget they have their role to play. If justice is to be a matter of persuasion, it cannot violate the deepest feelings we have (and have always had) about justice. If such violation takes place, the city will not thrive.

Every time I read the conclusion of this great trilogy, I think of how we nowadays may well have lost touch with that great insight: that justice is not just a matter of reasonable process and debate but also a matter of feeling. For a city to thrive justice must not only be reasonably done but must be felt to be done. Once our system starts to violate our feelings for justice, our city does not thrive. The Furies will see to that.

# The Legend of the Trojan War

## *by Ian Johnston*

This summary, which has been prepared by Ian Johnston of Malaspina University-College, Nanaimo, BC (now Vancouver Island University), for students in Classics 101 and Liberal Studies, is a brief account of a number of different old stories about the Trojan war, arranged in more or less chronological sequence. There are several different, even contradictory, versions of events. There is no one authoritative narrative of the whole war. Many of these stories were obviously current before Homer, and the story continued to be embellished by the Romans and Medieval writers]

1.  The gods Apollo and Poseidon, during a time when they were being punished by having to work among men, built the city of Troy for Priam's father, Laomedon. They invited the mortal man Aeacus (the son of Zeus and Aegina and grandfather of Achilles) to help them, since destiny had decreed that Troy would one day be captured in a place built by human hands (so a human being had to help them).

2.  When newly constructed, Troy was attacked and captured by Herakles (Hercules), Telamon (brother of Peleus and therefore the uncle of Achilles and father of Telamonian Ajax and Teucros), and Peleus (son of Aeacus and father of Achilles), as a punishment for the fact that Laomedon had not given Hercules a promised reward of immortal horses for rescuing Laomedon's daughter Hesione. Telamon killed Laomedon and took Hesione as a concubine (she was the mother of Teucros).

3.  Priam, King of Troy and son of Laomedon, had a son from his wife Hekabe (or Hecuba), who dreamed that she had given birth to a flaming torch. Cassandra, the prophetic daughter of Priam, foretold that the new-born son, Paris (also called Alexandros or Alexander), should be killed at birth or else he would destroy the city. Paris was taken out to be killed, but he was rescued by shepherds and grew up away from the city in the farms by Mount Ida. As a young man he returned to Troy to compete in the athletic games, was recognized, and returned to the royal family.

4.  Peleus (father of Achilles) fell in love with the sea nymph Thetis, whom Zeus, the most powerful of the gods, also had designs upon.

But Zeus learned of an ancient prophecy that Thetis would give birth to a son greater than his father, so he gave his divine blessing to the marriage of Peleus, a mortal king, and Thetis. All the gods were invited to the celebration, except, by a deliberate oversight, Eris, the goddess of strife. She came anyway and brought a golden apple, upon which was written "For the fairest." Hera (Zeus's wife), Aphrodite (Zeus's daughter), and Athena (Zeus's daughter) all made a claim for the apple, and they appealed to Zeus for judgment. He refused to adjudicate a beauty contest between his wife and two of his daughters, and the task of choosing a winner fell to Paris (while he was still a herdsman on Mount Ida, outside Troy). The goddesses each promised Paris a wonderful prize if he would pick her: Hera offered power, Athena offered military glory and wisdom, and Aphrodite offered him the most beautiful woman in the world as his wife. In the famous Judgement of Paris, Paris gave the apple to Aphrodite.

5. Helen, daughter of Tyndareus and Leda, was also the daughter of Zeus, who had made love to Leda in the shape of a swan (she is the only female child of Zeus and a mortal). Her beauty was famous throughout the world. Her father Tyndareus would not agree to any man's marrying her, until all the Greeks warrior leaders made a promise that they would collectively avenge any insult to her. When the leaders made such an oath, Helen then married Menelaus, King of Sparta. Her twin (non-divine) sister Klytaimnestra (Clytaemnestra), born at the same time as Helen but not a daughter of Zeus, married Agamemnon, King of Argos, and brother of Menelaus. Agamemnon was the most powerful leader in Hellas (Greece).

6. Paris, back in the royal family at Troy, made a journey to Sparta as a Trojan ambassador, at a time when Menelaus was away. Paris and Helen fell in love and left Sparta together, taking with them a vast amount of the city's treasure and returning to Troy via Cranae, an island off Attica, Sidon, and Egypt, among other places. The Spartans set off in pursuit but could not catch the lovers. When the Spartans learned that Helen and Paris were back in Troy, they sent a delegation (Odysseus, King of Ithaca, and Menelaus, the injured husband) to Troy demanding the return of Helen and the treasure. When the Trojans refused, the Spartans appealed to the oath which Tyndareus had forced them all to take (see 5 above), and the Greeks assembled an army to invade Troy, asking all the allies to meet in preparation for embarkation at Aulis. Some stories claimed that the real Helen never went to Troy, for she was carried off to Egypt by the god Hermes, and Paris took her double to Troy.

7.  Achilles, the son of Peleus and Thetis, was educated as a young man by Chiron, the centaur (half man and half horse). One of the conditions of Achilles's parents' marriage (the union of a mortal with a divine sea nymph) was that the son born to them would die in war and bring great sadness to his mother. To protect him from death in battle his mother bathed the infant in the waters of the river Styx, which conferred invulnerability to any weapon. And when the Greeks began to assemble an army, Achilles's parents hid him at Scyros disguised as a girl. While there he met Deidameia, and they had a son Neoptolemos (also called Pyrrhus). Calchas, the prophet with the Greek army, told Agamemnon and the other leaders that they could not conquer Troy without Achilles. Odysseus found Achilles by tricking him; Odysseus placed a weapon out in front of the girls of Scyros, and Achilles reached for it, thus revealing his identity. Menoitios, a royal counsellor, sent his son Patroclus to accompany Achilles on the expedition as his friend and advisor.

8.  The Greek fleet of one thousand ships assembled at Aulis. Agamemnon, who led the largest contingent, was the commander-in-chief. The army was delayed for a long time by contrary winds, and the future of the expedition was threatened as the forces lay idle. Agamemnon had offended the goddess Artemis by an impious boast, and Artemis had sent the winds. Finally, in desperation to appease the goddess, Agamemnon sacrificed his daughter Iphigeneia. Her father lured her to Aulis on the pretext that she was to be married to Achilles (whose earlier marriage was not known), but then he sacrificed her on the high altar. One version of her story claims that Artemis saved her at the last minute and carried her off to Tauris where she became a priestess of Artemis in charge of human sacrifices. While there, she later saved Orestes and Pylades. In any case, after the sacrifice Artemis changed the winds, and the fleet sailed for Troy.

9.  On the way to Troy, Philoctetes, the son of Poeas and leader of the seven ships from Methone, suffered a snake bite when the Greeks landed at Tenedos to make a sacrifice. His pain was so great and his wound so unpleasant (especially the smell) that the Greek army abandoned him against his will on the island.

10. The Greek army landed on the beaches before Troy. The first man ashore, Protesilaus, was killed by Hector, son of Priam and leader of the Trojan army. The Greeks sent another embassy to Troy, seeking to recover Helen and the treasure. When the Trojans denied them, the Greek army settled down into a siege which lasted many years.

11. In the tenth year of the war (where the narrative of the *Iliad* begins), Agamemnon insulted Apollo by taking as a slave-hostage the girl Chryseis, the daughter of Chryses, a prophet of Apollo, and refusing to return her when her father offered compensation. In revenge, Apollo sent nine days of plague down upon the Greek army. Achilles called an assembly to determine what the Greeks should do. In that assembly, he and Agamemnon quarrelled bitterly, Agamemnon confiscated from Achilles his slave girl Briseis, and Achilles, in a rage, withdrew himself and his forces (the Myrmidons) from any further participation in the war. He asked his mother, Thetis, the divine sea nymph, to intercede on his behalf with Zeus to give the Trojans help in battle, so that the Greek forces would recognize how foolish Agamemnon had been to offend the best soldier under his command. Thetis made the request of Zeus, reminding him of a favour she had once done for him, warning him about a revolt against his authority, and he agreed.

12. During the course of the war, numerous incidents took place, and many died on both sides. Paris and Menelaus fought a duel, and Aphrodite saved Paris just as Menelaus was about to kill him. Achilles, the greatest of the Greek warriors, slew Cycnus, Troilus, and many others. He also, according to various stories, was a lover of Patroclus, Troilus, Polyxena, daughter of Priam, Helen, and Medea. Odysseus and Diomedes slaughtered thirteen Thracians (Trojan allies) and stole the horses of King Rhesus in a night raid. Telamonian Ajax (the Greater Ajax) and Hector fought a duel with no decisive result. A common soldier, Thersites, challenged the authority of Agamemnon and demanded that the soldiers abandon the expedition. Odysseus beat Thersites into obedience. In the absence of Achilles and following Zeus's promise to Thetis (see 11), Hector enjoyed great success against the Greeks, breaking through their defensive ramparts on the beach and setting the ships on fire

13. While Hector was enjoying his successes against the Greeks, the latter sent an embassy to Achilles, requesting him to return to battle. Agamemnon offered many rewards in compensation for his initial insult (see 11). Achilles refused the offer but did say that he would reconsider if Hector ever reached the Greek ships. When Hector did so, Achilles's friend Patroclus (see 7) begged to be allowed to return to the fight. Achilles gave him permission, advising Patroclus not to attack the city of Troy itself. He also gave Patroclus his own suit of armour, so that the Trojans might think that Achilles had returned to the war. Patroclus resumed the fight, enjoyed some dazzling success

(killing one of the leaders of the Trojan allies, Sarpedon from Lykia), but he was finally killed by Hector, with the help of Apollo.

14. In his grief over the death of his friend Patroclus, Achilles decided to return to the battle. Since he had no armour (Hector had stripped the body of Patroclus and had put on the armour of Achilles), Thetis asked the divine artisan Hephaestus, the crippled god of the forge, to prepare some divine armour for her son. Hephaestus did so, Thetis gave the armour to Achilles, and he returned to the war. After slaughtering many Trojans, Achilles finally cornered Hector alone outside the walls of Troy. Hector chose to stand and fight rather than to retreat into the city, and he was killed by Achilles, who then mutilated the corpse, tied it to his chariot, and dragged it away. Achilles built a huge funeral pyre for Patroclus, killed Trojan soldiers as sacrifices, and organized the funeral games in honour of his dead comrade. Priam travelled to the Greek camp to plead for the return of Hector's body, and Achilles relented and returned it to Priam in exchange for a ransom.

15. In the tenth year of the war the Amazons, led by Queen Penthesilea, joined the Trojan forces. She was killed in battle by Achilles, as was King Memnon of Ethiopa, who had also recently reinforced the Trojans. Achilles's career as the greatest warrior came to an end when Paris, with the help of Apollo, killed him with an arrow which pierced him in the heel, the one vulnerable spot, which the waters of the River Styx had not touched because his mother had held him by the foot (see 7) when she had dipped the infant Achilles in the river. Telamonian Ajax, the second greatest Greek warrior after Achilles, fought valiantly in defense of Achilles's corpse. At the funeral of Achilles, the Greeks sacrificed Polyxena, the daughter of Hecuba, wife of Priam. After the death of Achilles, Odysseus and Telamonian Ajax fought over who should get the divine armour of the dead hero. When Ajax lost the contest, he went mad and committed suicide. In some versions, the Greek leaders themselves vote and decide to award the armour to Odysseus.

16. The Greeks captured Helenus, a son of Priam, and one of the chief prophets in Troy. Helenus revealed to the Greeks that they could not capture Troy without the help of Philoctetes, who owned the bow and arrows of Hercules and whom the Greeks had abandoned on Tenedos (see 9 above). Odysseus and Neoptolemus (the son of Achilles) set out to persuade Philoctetes, who was angry at the Greeks for leaving him alone on the island, to return to the war, and by trickery they

succeeded. Philoctetes killed Paris with an arrow shot from the bow of Hercules.

17. Odysseus and Diomedes ventured into Troy at night, in disguise, and stole the Palladium, the sacred statue of Athena, which was supposed to give the Trojans the strength to continue the war. The city, however, did not fall. Finally the Greeks devised the strategy of the wooden horse filled with armed soldiers. It was built by Epeius and left in front of Troy. The Greek army then withdrew to Tenedos (an island off the coast), as if abandoning the war. Odysseus went into Troy disguised, and Helen recognized him. But he was sent away by Hecuba, the wife of Priam, after Helen told her. The Greek soldier Sinon stayed behind when the army withdrew and pretended to the Trojans that he had deserted from the Greek army because he had information about a murder Odysseus had committed. He told the Trojans that the horse was an offering to Athena and that the Greeks had built it to be so large that the Trojans could not bring it into their city. The Trojan Laocoon warned the Trojans not to believe Sinon ("I fear the Greeks even when they bear gifts"); in the midst of his warnings a huge sea monster came from the surf and killed Laocoon and his sons.

18. The Trojans determined to get the Trojan Horse into their city. They tore down a part of the wall, dragged the horse inside, and celebrated their apparent victory. At night, when the Trojans had fallen asleep, the Greek soldiers hidden in the horse came out, opened the gates, and gave the signal to the main army which had been hiding behind Tenedos. The city was totally destroyed. King Priam was slaughtered at the altar by Achilles's son Neoptolemos. Hector's infant son, Astyanax, was thrown off the battlements. The women were taken prisoner: Hecuba (wife of Priam), Cassandra (daughter of Priam), and Andromache (wife of Hector). Helen was returned to Menelaus.

19. The gods regarded the sacking of Troy and especially the treatment of the temples as a sacrilege, and they punished many of the Greek leaders. The fleet was almost destroyed by a storm on the journey back. Menelaus's ships sailed all over the sea for seven years—to Egypt (where, in some versions, he recovered his real wife in the court of King Proteus—see 6 above). Agamemnon returned to Argos, where he was murdered by his wife Clytaemnestra and her lover, Aegisthus. Cassandra, whom Agamemnon had claimed as a concubine after the destruction of Troy, was also killed by Clytaemnestra. Aegisthus was seeking revenge for what the father of Agamemnon (Atreus) had

done to his brother (Aegisthus' father) Thyestes. Atreus had given a feast for Thyestes in which he fed to him the cooked flesh of his own children (see the family tree of the House of Atreus given below). Clytaemnestra claimed that she was seeking revenge for the sacrifice of her daughter Iphigeneia (see 8 above).

20. Odysseus (called by the Romans Ulysses) wandered over the sea for many years before reaching home. He started with a number of ships, but in a series of misfortunes, lasting ten years because of the enmity of Poseidon, the god of the sea, he lost all his men before returning to Ithaca alone. His adventures took him from Troy to Ismareos (land of the Cicones); to the land of the Lotos Eaters, the island of the cyclops (Poseidon, the god of the sea, became Odysseus's enemy when Odysseus put out the eye of Polyphemus, the cannibal cyclops, who was a son of Poseidon); to the cave of Aeolos (god of the winds), to the land of the Laestrygonians, to the islands of Circe and Calypso, to the underworld (where he talked to the ghost of Achilles); to the land of the Sirens, past the monster Scylla and the whirlpool Charybdis, to the pastures of the cattle of Helios, the sun god, to Phaiacia. Back in Ithaca in disguise, with the help of his son Telemachus and some loyal servants, he killed the young princes who had been trying to persuade his wife, Penelope, to marry one of them and who had been wasting the treasure of the palace and trying to kill Telemachus. Odysseus proved who he was by being able to string the famous bow of Odysseus, a feat which no other man could manage, and by describing for Penelope the secret of their marriage bed, that Odysseus had built it around an old olive tree.

21. After the murder of Agamemnon by his wife Clytaemnestra (see 19 above), his son Orestes returned with a friend Pylades to avenge his father. With the help of his sister Electra (who had been very badly treated by her mother, left either unmarried or married to a poor farmer so that she would have no royal children), Orestes killed his mother and Aegisthus. Then he was pursued by the Furies, the goddesses of blood revenge. Suffering fits of madness, Orestes fled to Delphi, then to Tauri, where, in some versions, he met his long-lost sister, Iphigeneia. She had been rescued from Agamemnon's sacrifice by the gods and made a priestess of Diana in Tauri. Orestes escaped with Iphigeneia to Athens. There he was put on trial for the matricide. Apollo testified in his defense. The jury vote was even; Athena cast the deciding vote in Orestes's favour. The outraged Furies were placated by being given a permanent place in Athens and a certain authority in the judicial process. They were then renamed the Eumenides (The

Kindly Ones). Orestes was later tried for the same matricide in Argos, at the insistence of Tyndareus, Clytaemnestra's father. Orestes and Electra were both sentenced to death by stoning. Orestes escaped by capturing Helen and using her as a hostage.

22. Neoptolemus, the only son of Achilles, married Hermione, the only daughter of Helen and Menelaus. Neoptolemus also took as a wife the widow of Hector, Andromache. There was considerable jealously between the two women. Orestes had wished to marry Hermione; by a strategy he arranged it so that the people of Delphi killed Neoptolemus. Then he carried off Hermione and married her. Menelaus tried to kill the son of Neoptolemus, Molossus, and Andromache, but Peleus, Achilles's father, rescued them. Andromache later married Helenus. Orestes's friend Pylades married Electra, Orestes sister.

23. Aeneas, the son of Anchises and the goddess Aphrodite and one of the important Trojan leaders in the Trojan War, fled from the city while the Greeks were destroying it, carrying his father, Anchises, his son Ascanius, and his ancestral family gods with him. Aeneas wandered all over the Mediterranean. On his journey to Carthage, he had an affair with Dido, Queen of Carthage. He abandoned her without warning, in accordance with his mission to found another city. Dido committed suicide in grief. Aeneas reached Italy and there fought a war against Turnus, the leader of the local Rutulian people. He did not found Rome but Lavinium, the main centre of the Latin league, from which the people of Rome sprang. Aeneas thus links the royal house of Troy with the Roman republic.

## *The Cultural Influence of the Legend of the Trojan War*

No story in our culture, with the possible exception of the Old Testament and the story of Jesus Christ, has inspired writers and painters over the centuries more than the Trojan War. It was the fundamental narrative in Greek education (especially in the version passed down by Homer, which covers only a small part of the total narrative), and all the tragedians whose works survive wrote plays upon various aspects of it, and these treatments, in turn, helped to add variations to the traditional story. No one authoritative work defines all the details of the story outlined above.

Unlike the Old Testament narratives, which over time became codified in a single authoritative version, the story of the Trojan War exists as a large collection of different versions of the same events (or parts of them). The war has been interpreted as a heroic tragedy, as a fanciful romance, as a satire against warfare, as a love story, as a passionately anti-war tale, and so on. Just as there is no single version which defines the "correct" sequence of events, so there is no single interpretative slant on how one should understand the war. Homer's poems enjoyed a unique authority, but they tell only a small part of the total story.

The following notes indicate only a few of the plays, novels, and poems which have drawn on and helped to shape this ancient story.

1. The most famous Greek literary stories of the war are Homer's *Iliad* and *Odyssey*, our first two epic poems, composed for oral recitation probably in the eighth century before Christ. The theme of the *Iliad* is the wrath of Achilles at the action of Agamemnon, and the epic follows the story of Achilles' withdrawal from the war and his subsequent return (see paragraphs 11, 12, 13, and 14 above). The *Odyssey* tells the story of the return of Odysseus from the war (see 20 above). A major reason for the extraordinary popularity and fecundity of the story of the Trojan War is the unquestioned quality and authority of these two great poems, even though they tell only a small part of the total narrative and were for a long time unavailable in Western Europe (after they were lost to the West, they did not appear until the fifteenth century). The *Iliad* was the inspiration for the archaeological work of Schliemann in the nineteenth century, a search which resulted in the discovery of the site of Troy at Hissarlik, in modern Turkey.

2. The Greek tragedians, we know from the extant plays and many fragments, found in the story of the Trojan War their favorite material, focusing especially on the events after the fall of the city. Aeschylus's famous trilogy, *The Oresteia* (*Agamemnon*, *Choephoroi* [*Libation Bearers*], and *Eumenides* [*The Kindly Ones*]), tells of the murder of Agamemnon and Cassandra by Clytaemnestra and Aegisthus, the revenge of Orestes, and the trial for the matricide. Both Sophocles and Euripides wrote plays about Electra, and Euripides also wrote a number of plays based on parts the larger story: *The Trojan Women*, *The Phoenissae*, *Orestes*, *Helen*, and *Iphigeneia in Tauris* (see 21 and 22 above). Sophocles also wrote *Philoctetes* (see 16) and *Ajax* (see 15) on events in the Trojan War.

3. Greek philosophers and historians used the Trojan War as a common example to demonstrate their own understanding of human conduct. So Herodotus and Thucydides, in defining their approach to the historical past, both offer an analysis of the origins of the war. Plato's *Republic* uses many parts of Homer's epics to establish important points about political wisdom (often citing Homer as a negative

# Aeschylus

example). Alexander the Great carried a copy of the *Iliad* around with him in a special royal casket which he had captured from Darius, King of the Persians.

4.  The Romans also adopted the story. Their most famous epic, Virgil's *Aeneid*, tells the story of Aeneas (see 23). And in the middle ages, the Renaissance, and right up to the present day, writers have retold parts of the ancient story. These adaptations often make significant changes in the presentation of particular characters, notably Achilles, who in many versions becomes a knightly lover, and Odysseus/Ulysses, who is often a major villain. Ulysses and Diomedes appear in Dante's *Inferno*. Of particular note are Chaucer's and Shakespeare's treatments of the story of Troilus and Cressida.

    Modern writers who have drawn on the literary tradition of this ancient cycle of stories include Sartre (*The Flies*), O'Neill (*Mourning Becomes Electra*), Giradoux (*Tiger at the Gates*), Joyce (*Ulysses*), Eliot, Auden, and many others. In addition, the story has formed the basis for operas and ballets, and the story of *Odysseus* has been made into a mini-series for television. This tradition is a complicated one, however, because many writers, especially in Medieval times, had no direct knowledge of the Greek sources and re-interpreted the details in very non-Greek ways (e.g., Dante, Chaucer, and Shakespeare). Homer's text, for example, was generally unknown in Western Europe until the late fifteenth century.

5.  For the past two hundred years there has been a steady increase in the popularity of Homer's poems (and other works dealing with parts of the legend) translated into English. Thus, in addition to the various modern adaptations of parts of the total legend of the Trojan war (e.g., Brad Pitt's *Troy*), the ancient versions are still very current.

## *The Royal House of Atreus*

The most famous (or notorious) human family in Western literature is the House of Atreus, the royal family of Mycenae. To follow the brief outline below, consult the simplified family tree on p. xxv. Note that different versions of the story offer modifications of the family tree.

The family of Atreus suffered from an ancestral crime, variously described. Most commonly Tantalus, son of Zeus and Pluto, stole the food of the gods. In another version he kills his son Pelops and feeds the flesh to the gods (who later, when they discover what they have eaten, bring Pelops back to life). Having eaten the food of the gods, Tantalus is immortal and so cannot be killed. In Homer's *Odyssey*, Tantalus is punished everlastingly in the underworld.

The family curse originates with Pelops, who won his wife Hippodamia in a chariot race by cheating and betraying and killing his co-conspirator (who, as he was drowning, cursed the family of Pelops). The curse blighted the next generation: the brothers Atreus and Thyestes quarrelled. Atreus killed Thyestes's sons and served them to their father at a reconciliation banquet.

To obtain revenge, Thyestes fathered a son on his surviving child, his daughter Pelopia. This child was Aegisthus, whose task it was to avenge the murder of his brothers. When Agamemnon set off for Troy (sacrificing his daughter Iphigeneia so that the fleet could sail from Aulis), Aegisthus seduced Clytaemnestra and established himself as a power in Argos.

When Agamemnon returned, Clytaemnestra and Aegisthus killed him (and his captive Cassandra)--Aegisthus in revenge for his brothers, Clytaemnestra in revenge for the sacrifice of Iphigeneia. Orestes at the time was away, and Electra had been disgraced.

Orestes returned to Argos to avenge his father. With the help of a friend, Pylades, and his sister Electra, he succeeded by killing his mother, Clytaemnestra, and her lover, Aegisthus. After many adventures (depending upon the narrative) he finally received absolution for the matricide, and the curse was over.

Many Greek poets focused on this story. Homer repeatedly mentions the murder of Agamemnon in the *Odyssey* and the revenge of Orestes on Aegisthus (paying no attention to the murder of Clytaemnestra); Aeschylus's great trilogy *The Oresteia* is the most famous classical treatment of the tale; Sophocles and Euripides both wrote plays on Orestes and Electra.

One curious note is the almost exact parallel between the story of Orestes in this family tale and the story of *Hamlet*. These two stories arose, it seems, absolutely independently of each other, and yet in many crucial respects are extraordinarily similar. This match has puzzled many a comparative literature scholar and invited all sorts of psychological theories about the trans-cultural importance of matricide as a theme.

For a more detailed account of the House of Atreus, see the following section.

# THE HOUSE OF ATREUS:
## A Note on the Mythological Background to the *Oresteia*
### *by Ian Johnston*

*Introduction*

    The following paragraphs provide a brief summary of the major events in the long history of the House of Atreus, one of the most fecund and long-lasting of all the Greek legends. Like so many other stories, the legend of the House of Atreus varies a good deal from one author to the next and there is no single authoritative version. The account given below tries to include as many of the major details as possible. At the end there is a short section reviewing Aeschylus' treatment of the story in the *Oresteia*.

*Family Tree (Simplified)*

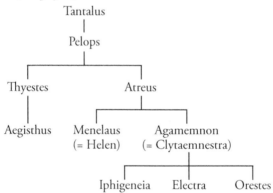

1. The family of Atreus (father of Agamemnon and Menelaus) traces its origins back to Tantalus, king of Sipylos, a son of Zeus (famous for his eternal punishment in Hades, as described in the *Odyssey*, where he is always thirsty but can never drink, hence the origin of the word *tantalizing*). Tantalus had a son called Pelops, whom Poseidon loved.

2. Pelops wished to marry Hippodameia, daughter of king Oenomaus. Oenomaus set up a contest (a chariot race against the king) for all those who wished to woo his daughter. If the suitor lost, he was killed. A number of men had died in such a race before Pelops made his attempt. Pelops bribed the king's charioteer (Myrtilus) to disable the

king's chariot. In the race, Oenomaus' chariot broke down (the wheels came off), and the king was killed. Pelops then carried off Hippodameia as his bride. Pelops also killed his co-conspirator Myrtilus by throwing him into the sea. Before he drowned Myrtilus (in some versions Oenomaus) cursed Pelops and his family. This act is the origin of the famous curse on the House of Atreus.

3. Pelops does not seems to have been affected by the curse. He had a number of children, the most important of whom were his two sons, the brothers Atreus and Thyestes. Atreus married Aerope, and they had two sons, Agamemnon and Menelaus. And Thyestes had two sons and a daughter Pelopia.

4. Atreus and Thyestes quarrelled (in some versions at the instigation of the god Hermes, father of Myrtilus, the charioteer killed by Pelops). Thyestes had an affair with Atreus' wife, Aerope, and was banished from Argos by Atreus. However, Thyestes petitioned to be allowed to return, and Atreus, apparently wishing a reconciliation, agreed to allow Thyestes to come back and prepared a huge banquet to celebrate the end of their differences.

5. At the banquet, however, Atreus served Thyestes the cooked flesh of Thyestes' two slaughtered sons. Thyestes ate the food, and then was informed of what he had done. This horrific event is the origin of the term *Thyestean Banquet*. Overcome with horror, Thyestes cursed the family of Atreus and left Argos with his one remaining child, his daughter Pelopia.

6. Some versions of the story include the name Pleisthenes, a son of Atreus who was raised by Thyestes. To become king, Thyestes sent Pleisthenes to kill Atreus, but Atreus killed him, not realizing he was killing his son. This, then, becomes another cause of the quarrel. In yet other accounts, someone called Pleisthenes is the first husband of Aerope and the father of Agamemnon and Menelaus. When he died, so this version goes, Atreus married Aerope and adopted her two sons. In Aeschylus' play there is one reference to Pleisthenes; otherwise, this ambiguous figure is absent from the story.

7. In some versions, including Aeschylus' account, Thyestes had one small infant son who survived the banquet, Aegisthus. In other accounts, however, Aegisthus was the product of Thyestes' incestuous relationship with his daughter Pelopia after the murder of the two older sons, conceived especially to be the avenger of the notorious banquet.

8. Agamemnon and Menelaus, the two sons of Atreus, married Clytaemnestra and Helen respectively, two twin sisters, but not identical twins (Clytaemnestra had a human father; whereas, Helen was a daughter of Zeus). Helen was so famous for her beauty that a number of men wished to marry her. The suitors all agreed that they would act to support the man she eventually married in the event of any need for mutual assistance. Agamemnon and Clytaemnestra had three children, Iphigeneia, Orestes, and Electra.

9. When Helen (Menelaus' wife) ran off to Troy with Paris, Agamemnon and Menelaus organized and led the Greek forces against the Trojans. The army assembled at Aulis, but the fleet could not sail because of contrary winds sent by Artemis. Agamemnon sacrificed his daughter Iphigeneia in order to placate Artemis.

10. With Agamemnon and Menelaus off in Troy, Aegisthus (son of Thyestes) returned to Argos, where he became the lover of Clytaemnestra, Agamemnon's wife. They sent Orestes into exile, to live with an ally, Strophius in Phocis, and humiliated Electra, Agamemnon's surviving daughter (either treating her as a servant or marrying her off to a common farmer). When Agamemnon returned, the two conspirators successfully killed him and assumed royal control of Argos.

11. Orestes returned from exile and, in collaboration with his sister Electra, avenged his father by killing Clytaemnestra and Aegisthus. In many versions this act makes him lose his self-control and he becomes temporarily deranged. He then underwent ritual purification by Apollo and sought refuge in the temple of Athena in Athens. There he was tried and acquitted. This action put the curses placed on the House of Atreus to rest.

## Some Comments

The story of the House of Atreus, and particularly Orestes' and Electra's revenge for their father's murder, is one of the most popular and enduring of all Greek legends, a favourite among the classical tragedians and still very popular with modern playwrights (e.g., T. S. Eliot, Eugene O'Neill, Jean Paul Sartre). However, different writers tell the story in very different ways.

Homer, for example (in the *Odyssey*) sets up Orestes' killing of Aegisthus as an entirely justified way to proceed (Homer ascribes the main motivation and planning to Aegisthus, who has to persuade Clytaemnestra to agree and who, it seems, does the actual killing). In fact, the action is repeatedly mentioned as a clear indication of divinely supported justice (there is no direct mention of the killing of Clytaemnestra, although there is a passing reference to Orestes' celebrations over his "hateful" mother after the killing of Aegisthus). Sophocles and Euripides tell basically the same story but with enormously different depictions of the main characters (in Euripides' version Orestes and Electra are hateful; whereas, in Sophocles' *Electra* they are much more conventionally righteous).

Aeschylus confines his attention to Atreus' crime against his brother (the Thyestean banquet) and what followed from it. There is no direct reference to Thyestes' adultery with Atreus' wife (although Cassandra makes a reference to a man sleeping with his brother's wife) or to any events from earlier parts of the story (unless the images of chariot racing are meant to carry an echo of Pelops' actions). This has the effect of making Atreus' crime against his brother the origin of the family curse (rather than the actions of Pelops or Tantalus) and tends to give the reader more sympathy for Aegisthus than some other versions do.

Curiously enough, Orestes' story has many close parallels with the Norse legend on which the story of Hamlet is based (son in exile is called upon to avenge a father killed by the man who has seduced his mother, perhaps with the mother's consent; the son carries out the act of killing his mother and her lover with great difficulty, undergoing fits of madness, and so on). Given that there is no suggestion of any possible literary-historical link between the origin of these two stories, the similarity of these plots offers a number of significant problems for psychologists and mythologists to explore. This puzzle is especially intriguing because the Hamlet-Orestes narrative is by far the most popular story in the history of English dramatic tragedy.

ΕΥΜΕΝΙΔΕΣ

EUMENIDES

# ΤΑ ΤΟΥ ΔΡΑΜΑΤΟΣ ΠΡΟΣΩΠΑ

ΠΥΘΙΑΣ ΠΡΟΦΗΤΙΣ

ΑΠΟΛΛΩΝ

ΟΡΕΣΤΗΣ

ΚΛΥΤΑΙΜΝΗΣΤΡΑ

ΧΟΡΟΣ ΕΥΜΕΝΙΔΩΝ

ΑΘΗΝΑ

ΠΡΟΠΟΜΠΟΙ

# DRAMATIS PERSONAE

PRIESTESS: prophetic priestess (the Pythia) of Apollo at Delphi.

APOLLO: divine son of Zeus, god of prophecy.

ORESTES: son of Agamemnon and Clytaemnestra, brother of Electra.

CLYTAEMNESTRA: mother of Orestes, appearing as a ghost after her murder.

CHORUS: Furies, goddesses of blood revenge.

ATHENA: divine daughter of Zeus who was born fully grown from his head (without a mother).

Escort of ATHENIAN CITIZENS

# Εὐμενίδες

ΠΥΘΙΑΣ

πρῶτον μὲν εὐχῇ τῇδε πρεσβεύω θεῶν
τὴν πρωτόμαντιν Γαῖαν· ἐκ δὲ τῆς Θέμιν,
ἣ δὴ τὸ μητρὸς δευτέρα τόδ᾽ ἕζετο
μαντεῖον, ὡς λόγος τις· ἐν δὲ τῷ τρίτῳ
λάχει, θελούσης, οὐδὲ πρὸς βίαν τινός,            5
Τιτανὶς ἄλλη παῖς Χθονὸς καθέζετο,
Φοίβη· δίδωσι δ᾽ ἣ γενέθλιον δόσιν
Φοίβῳ· τὸ Φοίβης δ᾽ ὄνομ᾽ ἔχει παρώνυμον.
λιπὼν δὲ λίμνην Δηλίαν τε χοιράδα,
κέλσας ἐπ᾽ ἀκτὰς ναυπόρους τὰς Παλλάδος,      10
ἐς τήνδε γαῖαν ἦλθε Παρνησοῦ θ᾽ ἕδρας.
πέμπουσι δ᾽ αὐτὸν καὶ σεβίζουσιν μέγα
κελευθοποιοὶ παῖδες Ἡφαίστου, χθόνα
ἀνήμερον τιθέντες ἡμερωμένην.
μολόντα δ᾽ αὐτὸν κάρτα τιμαλφεῖ λεώς,         15
Δελφός τε χώρας τῆσδε πρυμνήτης ἄναξ.
τέχνης δέ νιν Ζεὺς ἔνθεον κτίσας φρένα
ἵζει τέταρτον τοῖσδε μάντιν ἐν θρόνοις·
Διὸς προφήτης δ᾽ ἐστὶ Λοξίας πατρός.
τούτους ἐν εὐχαῖς φροιμιάζομαι θεούς.          20
Παλλὰς προναία δ᾽ ἐν λόγοις πρεσβεύεται·
σέβω δὲ νύμφας, ἔνθα Κωρυκὶς πέτρα
κοίλη, φίλορνις, δαιμόνων ἀναστροφή·
Βρόμιος ἔχει τὸν χῶρον, οὐδ᾽ ἀμνημονῶ,

4

## Eumenides

*[Scene: The play opens just in front of the temple of Apollo at Delphi]*

*[Enter the Pythia, the Priestess of Apollo]*

PRIESTESS

In my prayer, I hold Earth in highest honour,
as the first of prophets among all gods.
Then, after her came Themis. That goddess,
so the legend goes, followed her mother
at this seat of prophecy. Third in line,
another Titan, Phoebe, child of Earth,
was then assigned to occupy this throne.
There was no force—Themis approved the change.
Phoebe then gave it as a birthday gift
to the god who takes his name from her,
Phoebus Apollo. He left the island Delos,
moving from his lake and ridge to Pallas,                    [10]
to those shores where ships sail in to trade.
Then he came to live on Mount Parnassus.
A reverential escort came with him—
children of the fire god, Hephaestus,
highway builders who tame the wilderness
and civilize the land. As he marched here,
people came out in droves to worship him,
including their king and helmsman, Delphus.
Then Zeus inspired in him prophetic skills,
and set him on this throne as fourth in line.
Here Apollo speaks for Zeus, his father.
My prayers begin with preludes to these gods.               [20]
My words also give special prominence
to the goddess who stands outside the shrine,
Pallas Athena. I revere those nymphs
inhabiting Corycia's rocky caves,
where flocks of birds delight to congregate,
where holy spirits roam. I don't forget
how Dionysus, ruler of this land,

5

ἐξ οὗτε Βάκχαις ἐστρατήγησεν θεός,                    25
λαγὼ δίκην Πενθεῖ καταρράψας μόρον·
Πλειστοῦ τε πηγὰς καὶ Ποσειδῶνος κράτος
καλοῦσα καὶ τέλειον ὕψιστον Δία,
ἔπειτα μάντις ἐς θρόνους καθιζάνω.
καὶ νῦν τυχεῖν με τῶν πρὶν εἰσόδων μακρῷ        30
ἄριστα δοῖεν· κεἰ παρ' Ἑλλήνων τινές,
ἴτων πάλῳ λαχόντες, ὡς νομίζεται.
μαντεύομαι γὰρ ὡς ἂν ἡγῆται θεός.

ἦ δεινὰ λέξαι, δεινὰ δ' ὀφθαλμοῖς δρακεῖν,
πάλιν μ' ἔπεμψεν ἐκ δόμων τῶν Λοξίου,           35
ὡς μήτε σωκεῖν μήτε μ' ἀκταίνειν βάσιν,
τρέχω δὲ χερσίν, οὐ ποδωκείᾳ σκελῶν·
δείσασα γὰρ γραῦς οὐδέν, ἀντίπαις μὲν οὖν.

ἐγὼ μὲν ἕρπω πρὸς πολυστεφῆ μυχόν·
ὁρῶ δ' ἐπ' ὀμφαλῷ μὲν ἄνδρα θεομυσῆ            40
ἕδραν ἔχοντα προστρόπαιον, αἵματι
στάζοντα χεῖρας καὶ νεοσπαδὲς ξίφος
ἔχοντ' ἐλαίας θ' ὑψιγέννητον κλάδον,
λήνει μεγίστῳ σωφρόνως ἐστεμμένον,
ἀργῆτι μαλλῷ· τῇδε γὰρ τρανῶς ἐρῶ.             45
πρόσθεν δὲ τἀνδρὸς τοῦδε θαυμαστὸς λόχος
εὕδει γυναικῶν ἐν θρόνοισιν ἥμενος.
οὔτοι γυναῖκας, ἀλλὰ Γοργόνας λέγω,
οὐδ' αὖτε Γοργείοισιν εἰκάσω τύποις.
εἶδόν ποτ' ἤδη Φινέως γεγραμμένας               50
δεῖπνον φερούσας· ἄπτεροί γε μὴν ἰδεῖν

divine commander of those Bacchic women,
ripped Pentheus apart, as if he were
a cornered rabbit.[1] I also call upon
the streams of Pleistus and Poseidon's power,
and Zeus most high, who fulfills all things.
I'll take my seat now on the prophet's throne.
May I be fortunate, above the rest,                                    [30]
to see far more than previous attempts.
If any Greeks are in attendance here,
let them draw lots and enter, each in turn,
as is our custom. I will prophesy,
following directions from the god.

*[The Priestess enters the temple, only to return immediately, very agitated. She
collapses onto her hands and knees]*

                              It's horrible!
Too horrible to say . . . awful to see.
It drives me back . . . out of Apollo's shrine.
My strength is gone . . . I can't stand up.
I have to crawl on hands and knees—my legs
just buckle under me . . . An old woman
overcome with fear is nothing, a child.
No more . . .

*[The Priestess gathers herself together and stands with great difficulty, holding
onto the temple doors for support]*

                    As I was entering the inner shrine—
the part covered up with wreaths—I saw him,          [40]
right on the central navel stone, a man
the gods despise, sitting there, in the seat
reserved for suppliants, hands dripping blood.
He'd drawn his sword, but held an olive branch.
It had a tuft of wool on top, a mark
of reverence—a large one, really white.
I saw all that distinctly. But then I saw
in front of him something astonishing,
on the benches groups of women sleeping—
well, they weren't exactly women,
I'd say more like Gorgons—then again,
not much like Gorgons either. Years ago
I once saw a picture of some monsters
snatching a feast away from Phineas.          [50]
But the ones inside here have no wings—

7

αὗται, μέλαιναι δ' ἐς τὸ πᾶν βδελύκτροποι·
ῥέγκουσι δ' οὐ πλατοῖσι φυσιάμασιν·
ἐκ δ' ὀμμάτων λείβουσι δυσφιλῆ λίβα·
καὶ κόσμος οὔτε πρὸς θεῶν ἀγάλματα          55
φέρειν δίκαιος οὔτ' ἐς ἀνθρώπων στέγας.
τὸ φῦλον οὐκ ὄπωπα τῆσδ' ὁμιλίας
οὐδ' ἥτις αἶα τοῦτ' ἐπεύχεται γένος
τρέφουσ' ἀνατεὶ μὴ μεταστένειν πόνον.
τἀντεῦθεν ἤδη τῶνδε δεσπότῃ δόμων          60
αὐτῷ μελέσθω Λοξίᾳ μεγασθενεῖ.
ἰατρόμαντις δ' ἐστὶ καὶ τερασκόπος
καὶ τοῖσιν ἄλλοις δωμάτων καθάρσιος.

ΑΠΟΛΛΩΝ

οὔτοι προδώσω· διὰ τέλους δέ σοι φύλαξ
ἐγγὺς παρεστὼς καὶ πρόσω δ' ἀποστατῶν          65
ἐχθροῖσι τοῖς σοῖς οὐ γενήσομαι πέπων.
καὶ νῦν ἁλούσας τάσδε τὰς μάργους ὁρᾷς·
ὕπνῳ πεσοῦσαι δ' αἱ κατάπτυστοι κόραι,
γραῖαι παλαιαὶ παῖδες, αἷς οὐ μείγνυται
θεῶν τις οὐδ' ἄνθρωπος οὐδὲ θήρ ποτε.          70
κακῶν δ' ἕκατι κἀγένοντ', ἐπεὶ κακὸν
σκότον νέμονται Τάρταρόν θ' ὑπὸ χθονός,
μισήματ' ἀνδρῶν καὶ θεῶν Ὀλυμπίων.
ὅμως δὲ φεῦγε μηδὲ μαλθακὸς γένῃ.
ἐλῶσι γάρ σε καὶ δι' ἠπείρου μακρᾶς          75
βιβῶντ' ἀν' αἰεὶ τὴν πλανοστιβῆ χθόνα
ὑπέρ τε πόντον καὶ περιρρύτας πόλεις.
καὶ μὴ πρόκαμνε τόνδε βουκολούμενος
πόνον· μολὼν δὲ Παλλάδος ποτὶ πτόλιν
ἵζου παλαιὸν ἄγκαθεν λαβὼν βρέτας.          80
κἀκεῖ δικαστὰς τῶνδε καὶ θελκτηρίους

I checked. They're black and totally repulsive,
with loud rasping snorts that terrify me.
Disgusting pus comes oozing from their eyes.
As for their clothing—quite inappropriate
to wear before the statues of the gods,
or even in men's homes. I've never seen
a tribe which could produce this company,
a country which would admit with pride
that it had raised them without paying a price,
without regretting all the pain they cost.
Where does this end? That is Apollo's work.                    [60]
Let that be his concern. His force is strong—
what he reveals has healing power.
He reads the omens and can purify
the home, his own and other men's.

*[The scene changes to reveal the inside of the temple, with Orestes clutching the central stone (the navel stone) and the Furies asleep in front of him. Apollo enters from the back of the temple (the inner shrine). Apollo moves to stand near Orestes]*

APOLLO

I'll not leave you—no, I'll stand beside you,
your protector till the end. Close at hand
or far away, I'll show no gentleness
towards your enemies. Right now you see
these frenzied creatures overcome with sleep,
just lying there, these loathsome maidens,
ancient children, hags. No god or man                         [70]
or animal has intercourse with them.
They're born for evil. That's why they live
within the blackest gloom of Tartarus,
under the earth. Olympian gods and men
despise them. But you should still keep going.
Do not give up. They'll chase you everywhere,
as you move along well-traveled ground,
across wide continents, beyond the seas,
through cities with the ocean all around.
Don't grow weary brooding on your pain.
And then, once you reach Athena's city,
sit down, and wrap your arms around her,                       [80]
embrace her image. With people there
to judge your cause and with the force of speech,

9

Aeschylus

μύθους ἔχοντες μηχανὰς εὑρήσομεν,
ὥστ' ἐς τὸ πᾶν σε τῶνδ' ἀπαλλάξαι πόνων·
καὶ γὰρ κτανεῖν σ' ἔπεισα μητρῷον δέμας.

ΟΡΕΣΤΗΣ

ἄναξ Ἄπολλον, οἶσθα μὲν τὸ μὴ 'δικεῖν·    85
ἐπεὶ δ' ἐπίστᾳ, καὶ τὸ μὴ 'μελεῖν μάθε.
σθένος δὲ ποιεῖν εὖ φερέγγυον τὸ σόν.

ΑΠΟΛΛΩΝ

μέμνησο, μὴ φόβος σε νικάτω φρένας.
σὺ δ', αὐτάδελφον αἷμα καὶ κοινοῦ πατρός,
Ἑρμῆ, φύλασσε· κάρτα δ' ὢν ἐπώνυμος    90
πομπαῖος ἴσθι, τόνδε ποιμαίνων ἐμὸν
ἱκέτην—σέβει τοι Ζεὺς τόδ' ἐκνόμων σέβας—
ὁρμώμενον βροτοῖσιν εὐπόμπῳ τύχῃ.

ΚΛΥΤΑΙΜΗΣΤΡΑΣ ΕΙΔΩΛΟΝ

εὕδοιτ' ἄν, ὠή, καὶ καθευδουσῶν τί δεῖ;
ἐγὼ δ' ὑφ' ὑμῶν ὧδ' ἀπητιμασμένη    95
ἄλλοισιν ἐν νεκροῖσιν, ὧν μὲν ἔκτανον
ὄνειδος ἐν φθιτοῖσιν οὐκ ἐκλείπεται,
αἰσχρῶς δ' ἀλῶμαι· προυννέπω δ' ὑμῖν ὅτι
ἔχω μεγίστην αἰτίαν κείνων ὕπο·
παθοῦσα δ' οὕτω δεινὰ πρὸς τῶν φιλτάτων,    100
οὐδεὶς ὑπέρ μου δαιμόνων μηνίεται,
κατασφαγείσης πρὸς χερῶν μητροκτόνων.
ὁρᾶτε πληγὰς τάσδε καρδίας ὅθεν.
εὕδουσα γὰρ φρὴν ὄμμασιν λαμπρύνεται,
ἐν ἡμέρᾳ δὲ μοῖρ' ἀπρόσκοπος βροτῶν.    105
ἦ πολλὰ μὲν δὴ τῶν ἐμῶν ἐλείξατε,
χοάς τ' ἀοίνους, νηφάλια μειλίγματα,
καὶ νυκτίσεμνα δεῖπν' ἐπ' ἐσχάρᾳ πυρὸς
ἔθυον, ὥραν οὐδενὸς κοινὴν θεῶν.

10

the spell-binding power in words, we'll find
a way to free you from misfortune.
For I was the one who urged you on
to kill your mother.

ORESTES
My lord Apollo,
you have no knowledge how to be unjust.
That being the case, now learn compassion, too.
Your power to do good is strong enough.

APOLLO
Remember this—don't let fear defeat you
by conquering your spirit. And you, Hermes,                    [90]
my own blood brother from a common father,
protect this man. Live up to that name of yours,
and be his guide. Since he's my suppliant,
lead him as if you were his shepherd—
remember Zeus respects an outcast's rights—
with you to show the way, he'll get better,
and quickly come among men once again.

*[Exit Orestes. Apollo moves back into the inner sanctuary. Enter the Ghost of Clytaemnestra]*

GHOST OF CLYTAEMNESTRA *[addressing the sleeping chorus]*
Ah, you may be fast asleep, but now
what use is sleeping? On account of you,
I alone among the dead lack honour.
The ghosts of those I killed revile me—
they never stop. I wander in disgrace.
They charge me with the most horrific crimes.
But I, too, suffered cruelty from those                       [100]
most dear to me. And yet, although I died
at the hands of one who killed his mother,
no spirit is enraged on my behalf.
Look here—you see these slashes on my heart?
How did they get there? While it's asleep
the mind can see, but in the light of day
we have no vision of men's destiny.
You've licked up many of my offerings,
soothing milk and honey without wine.
I've given many sacrificial gifts
with fire in my hearth at solemn banquets,
in that night hour no god will ever share.

11

Aeschylus

καὶ πάντα ταῦτα λὰξ ὁρῶ πατούμενα.                    110
ὁ δ' ἐξαλύξας οἴχεται νεβροῦ δίκην,
καὶ ταῦτα κούφως ἐκ μέσων ἀρκυστάτων
ὤρουσεν ὑμῖν ἐγκατιλλώψας μέγα.
ἀκούσαθ' ὡς ἔλεξα τῆς ἐμῆς περὶ
ψυχῆς, φρονήσατ', ὦ κατὰ χθονὸς θεαί.                 115
ὄναρ γὰρ ὑμᾶς νῦν Κλυταιμήστρα καλῶ.

ΧΟΡΟΣ
( μυγμός. )

ΚΛΥΤΑΙΜΗΣΤΡΑΣ ΕΙΔΩΛΟΝ
μύζοιτ' ἄν, ἀνὴρ δ' οἴχεται φεύγων πρόσω·
φίλοι γάρ εἰσιν οὐκ ἐμοῖς προσεικότες.

ἄγαν ὑπνώσσεις κοὐ κατοικτίζεις πάθος·          120
φονεὺς δ' Ὀρέστης τῆσδε μητρὸς οἴχεται.

ᾤζεις, ὑπνώσσεις· οὐκ ἀναστήσῃ τάχος;
τί σοι πέπρωται πρᾶγμα πλὴν τεύχειν κακά;       125

ὕπνος πόνος τε κύριοι συνωμόται
δεινῆς δρακαίνης ἐξεκήραναν μένος.

ΧΟΡΟΣ
( μυγμὸς διπλοῦς ὀξύς. )
λαβὲ λαβὲ λαβὲ λαβέ, φράζου.                         130

ΚΛΥΤΑΙΜΗΣΤΡΑΣ ΕΙΔΩΛΟΝ
ὄναρ διώκεις θῆρα, κλαγγαίνεις δ' ἅπερ
κύων μέριμναν οὔποτ' ἐκλείπων πόνου.
τί δρᾷς; ἀνίστω, μή σε νικάτω πόνος,
μηδ' ἀγνοήσῃς πῆμα μαλθαχθεῖσ' ὕπνῳ.
ἄλγησον ἧπαρ ἐνδίκοις ὀνείδεσιν·                   135
τοῖς σώφροσιν γὰρ ἀντίκεντρα γίγνεται.
σὺ δ' αἱματηρὸν πνεῦμ' ἐπουρίσασα τῷ,
ἀτμῷ κατισχναίνουσα, νηδύος πυρί,
ἕπου, μάραινε δευτέροις διώγμασιν.

12

I see all that being trampled underfoot.              [110]
He's gone, eluded you—just like a fawn,
he's jumped the centre of your nets with ease.
He mocks your efforts as he moves away.
Listen to me. I'm speaking of my soul.
So rouse yourselves! Wake up, you goddesses
from underground. While you dream on I call—
now Clytaemnestra summons you!

*[The members of the Chorus begin to make strange sounds and to mutter in their sleep]*

You may well moan—the man's escaped. He's gone.       [120]
He's flown a long way off. The friends he has
are stronger than my own. You sleep on there
so heavily, no sense of my distress.
Orestes, the man who killed his mother,
has run off! You mutter, but keep sleeping.
On your feet!. Why won't you get up? What work
has fate assigned you if not causing pain?
Sleep and hard work, two apt confederates,
have made these fearsome dragons impotent,
draining all their rage.

CHORUS MEMBER *[muttering in her sleep]*
                                        Seize him!
Seize him! Seize him! Seize that man! Look out!       [130]

GHOST OF CLYTAEMNESTRA
You hunt your prey, but only in your dreams,
whimpering like hounds who never lose
their keenness for the hunt. But you don't act!
Get up! Don't let exhaustion beat you down.
Sleep makes you soft—you overlook my pain.
Let my reproaches justly prick your hearts,
a spur for those who act with righteousness.
Blow your blood-filled breath all over him.
Let those fires in your bodies shrivel him.
Go on! Drive him to a fresh pursuit. Go!

13

ΧΟΡΟΣ

ἔγειρ', ἔγειρε καὶ σὺ τήνδ', ἐγὼ δὲ σέ.　　　140
εὕδεις; ἀνίστω, κἀπολακτίσασ' ὕπνον,
ἰδώμεθ' εἴ τι τοῦδε φροιμίου ματᾷ.

— ἰοὺ ἰοὺ πύπαξ. ἐπάθομεν, φίλαι,

— ἦ πολλὰ δὴ παθοῦσα καὶ μάτην ἐγώ,

— ἐπάθομεν πάθος δυσαχές, ὦ πόποι,　　　145
ἄφερτον κακόν·

— ἐξ ἀρκύων πέπτωκεν οἴχεταί θ' ὁ θήρ.
ὕπνῳ κρατηθεῖσ' ἄγραν ὤλεσα.

— ἰὼ παῖ Διός, ἐπίκλοπος πέλῃ,

— νέος δὲ γραίας δαίμονας καθιππάσω,　　　150

— τὸν ἱκέταν σέβων, ἄθεον ἄνδρα καὶ
τοκεῦσιν πικρόν·

— τὸν μητραλοίαν δ' ἐξέκλεψας ὢν θεός.

— τί τῶνδ' ἐρεῖ τις δικαίως ἔχειν;

— ἐμοὶ δ' ὄνειδος ἐξ ὀνειράτων μολὸν　　　155
ἔτυψεν δίκαν διφρηλάτου
μεσολαβεῖ κέντρῳ
ὑπὸ φρένας, ὑπὸ λοβόν.

— πάρεστι μαστίκτορος δαΐου δαμίου　　　160
βαρὺ τὸ περίβαρυ κρύος ἔχειν.

— τοιαῦτα δρῶσιν οἱ νεώτεροι θεοί,
κρατοῦντες τὸ πᾶν δίκας πλέον

14

*[The Furies begin to wake up slowly, one after the other. As they start to get up, the Ghost of Clytaemnestra exits]*

CHORUS LEADER *[waking up and rousing the other Furies]*
Wake up! Come on, I'll wake you up.                    [140]
Now do the same for her. Still sleeping?
Stand up. Wipe that sleep out of your eyes.
Let's chant our prelude—that should take effect.

*[The Furies, now awake, gather as a group, moving around trying to find Orestes or smell his track. They speak these lines as individual members of the larger group]*

— Ah ha, what this? Dear sisters, something's wrong.

— I've been through a lot, and all for nothing.

— We're being made to suffer something bad,
alas, an evil we cannot endure.

— Our quarry's slipped our nets. He's gone!
Once sleep came over us, we lost our prey.

— You're disgraceful, Hermes, a child of Zeus
who loves to steal.

                    — For a god you're young—                    [150]
but still you trample on more ancient spirits.

— You showed that suppliant respect,
a godless man, so vicious to his parent.

— You may be a god, but you're a thief.
You filched a man who killed his mother.

— Who can say there's justice in such theft?

— In my dreams shame struck—
it came on like a charioteer
who gripped his cruel whip so tight,
then hit under my heart,
deep in my gut.

— I feel the executioner's scourge,                    [160]
the one who wields a heavy lash,
weighed down with pain.

— Younger gods are doing this—
they push their ruling power
beyond what's theirs by right.

15

— φονολιβῆ θρόνον

περὶ πόδα, περὶ κάρα.                                                 165

— πάρεστι γᾶς ὀμφαλὸν προσδρακεῖν αἱμάτων

βλοσυρὸν ἀρόμενον ἄγος ἔχειν.

— ἐφεστίῳ δὲ μάντις ὢν μιάσματι

μυχὸν ἐχράνατ᾽ αὐτόσσυτος, αὐτόκλητος,                170

παρὰ νόμον θεῶν βρότεα μὲν τίων,

— παλαιγενεῖς δὲ μοίρας φθίσας.

— κἀμοί γε λυπρός, καὶ τὸν οὐκ ἐκλύσεται,

ὑπό τε γᾶν φυγὼν οὔ ποτ᾽ ἐλευθεροῦται.               175

— ποτιτρόπαιος ὢν δ᾽ ἕτερον ἐν κάρᾳ

μιάστορ᾽ ἐκ γένους πάσεται.

ΑΠΟΛΛΩΝ

ἔξω, κελεύω, τῶνδε δωμάτων τάχος

χωρεῖτ᾽, ἀπαλλάσσεσθε μαντικῶν μυχῶν,                180

μὴ καὶ λαβοῦσα πτηνὸν ἀργηστὴν ὄφιν,

χρυσηλάτου θώμιγγος ἐξορμώμενον,

ἀνῇς ὑπ᾽ ἄλγους μέλαν ἀπ᾽ ἀνθρώπων ἀφρόν,

ἐμοῦσα θρόμβους οὓς ἀφείλκυσας φόνου.

οὔτοι δόμοισι τοῖσδε χρίμπτεσθαι πρέπει·             185

ἀλλ᾽ οὗ καρανιστῆρες ὀφθαλμωρύχοι

δίκαι σφαγαί τε σπέρματός τ᾽ ἀποφθορᾷ

παίδων κακοῦται χλοῦνις, ἠδ᾽ ἀκρωνία,

λευσμός τε, καὶ μύζουσιν οἰκτισμὸν πολὺν

ὑπὸ ῥάχιν παγέντες. ἆρ᾽ ἀκούετε                      190

οἵας ἑορτῆς ἔστ᾽ ἀπόπτυστοι θεοῖς

στέργηθρ᾽ ἔχουσαι; πᾶς δ᾽ ὑφηγεῖται τρόπος

— Their throne drips blood
   around its foot,
   around its head.

— I see Earth's central navel stone
   defiled with blood, corrupted,
   stained with guilt.[2]

— The prophet soils the hearth,
   pollutes the shrine himself,                    [170]
   acting on his own behalf.
   against divine tradition,
   he honours human things.

— He sets aside decrees of fate
   established long ago.

— Though he inflict his pain on me,
   he'll never free that man.
   Let him flee underground,
   he'll find no liberty below.

— As he seeks to cleanse himself
   he'll meet the next avenger—
   a family member coming for his head.

*[Enter Apollo from the inner part of the shrine]*

APOLLO
   Get out! I'm ordering you to leave this house.
   Move on! Out of my prophet's sanctuary!          [180]
   Go now, or else you'll feel my arrows bite,
   glittering winged snakes shot from a golden string.
   Then, your agonies will make you choke,
   spit out black froth you suck from men,
   and vomit up the clotted blood you've drunk
   from murder. This shrine's no place for you.
   No, you belong where heads are sliced away,
   eyes gouged out—where justice equals slaughter—
   where youthful men are ruined by castration,
   where others suffer mutilation, stoning,
   where men impaled on spikes below the spine
   scream all the time. That's the feast you love.    [190]
   You hear me? And that's why gods detest you.
   The way you look, your shape, says what you are—

17

μορφῆς. λέοντος ἄντρον αἱματορρόφου
οἰκεῖν τοιαύτας εἰκός, οὐ χρηστηρίοις
ἐν τοῖσδε πλησίοισι τρίβεσθαι μύσος.      195
χωρεῖτ᾽ ἄνευ βοτῆρος αἰπολούμεναι.
ποίμνης τοιαύτης δ᾽ οὔτις εὐφιλὴς θεῶν.

ΧΟΡΟΣ
ἄναξ Ἄπολλον, ἀντάκουσον ἐν μέρει.
αὐτὸς σὺ τούτων οὐ μεταίτιος πέλῃ,
ἀλλ᾽ εἰς τὸ πᾶν ἔπραξας ὢν παναίτιος.      200

ΑΠΟΛΛΩΝ
πῶς δή; τοσοῦτο μῆκος ἔκτεινον λόγου.

ΧΟΡΟΣ
ἔχρησας ὥστε τὸν ξένον μητροκτονεῖν.

ΑΠΟΛΛΩΝ
ἔχρησα ποινὰς τοῦ πατρὸς πρᾶξαι. τί μήν;

ΧΟΡΟΣ
κἄπειθ᾽ ὑπέστης αἵματος δέκτωρ νέου.

ΑΠΟΛΛΩΝ
καὶ προστραπέσθαι τούσδ᾽ ἐπέστελλον δόμους.      205

ΧΟΡΟΣ
καὶ τὰς προπομποὺς δῆτα τάσδε λοιδορεῖς;

ΑΠΟΛΛΩΝ
οὐ γὰρ δόμοισι τοῖσδε πρόσφορον μολεῖν.

ΧΟΡΟΣ
ἀλλ᾽ ἔστιν ἡμῖν τοῦτο προστεταγμένον.

ΑΠΟΛΛΩΝ
τίς ἥδε τιμή; κόμπασον γέρας καλόν.

ΧΟΡΟΣ
τοὺς μητραλοίας ἐκ δόμων ἐλαύνομεν.      210

18

some blood-soaked lion's den might be your home.
You must not infect those near this temple
with your pollution. So leave this place,
you flock without a shepherd, you herd
the gods despise.

CHORUS LEADER

                    Lord Apollo,
listen to what we say. It's our turn to speak.
You're no mere accomplice in this crime—
you did it all yourself. You bear the guilt.                    [200]

APOLLO
What does that mean? Go on. Keep talking.

CHORUS LEADER
You told that stranger to kill his mother.

APOLLO
To avenge his father is what I said.
What's wrong with that?

CHORUS LEADER
                    Then you supported him.
You helped a man who'd just committed murder.

APOLLO
And I instructed him to come back here
to expiate his crime.

CHORUS LEADER
                    Then why insult us,
the ones who chased him here?

APOLLO
                    It's not right
for you to come inside my shrine.

CHORUS LEADER
We've been assigned to do this.

APOLLO
                    Assigned?
What's that? Proclaim your fine authority.

CHORUS LEADER
We chase out of their homes those criminals                    [210]
who slaughter their own mothers.

19

ΑΠΟΛΛΩΝ

τί γὰρ γυναικὸς ἥτις ἄνδρα νοσφίσῃ;

ΧΟΡΟΣ

οὐκ ἂν γένοιθ᾽ ὅμαιμος αὐθέντης φόνος.

ΑΠΟΛΛΩΝ

ἦ κάρτ᾽ ἄτιμα καὶ παρ᾽ οὐδὲν εἰργάσω
Ἥρας τελείας καὶ Διὸς πιστώματα.
Κύπρις δ᾽ ἄτιμος τῷδ᾽ ἀπέρριπται λόγῳ,                    215
ὅθεν βροτοῖσι γίγνεται τὰ φίλτατα.
εὐνὴ γὰρ ἀνδρὶ καὶ γυναικὶ μόρσιμος
ὅρκου 'στὶ μείζων τῇ δίκῃ φρουρουμένη.
εἰ τοῖσιν οὖν κτείνουσιν ἀλλήλους χαλᾷς
τὸ μὴ τίνεσθαι μηδ᾽ ἐποπτεύειν κότῳ,                      220
οὔ φημ᾽ Ὀρέστην σ᾽ ἐνδίκως ἀνδρηλατεῖν.
τὰ μὲν γὰρ οἶδα κάρτα σ᾽ ἐνθυμουμένην,
τὰ δ᾽ ἐμφανῶς πράσσουσαν ἡσυχαιτέραν.
δίκας δὲ Παλλὰς τῶνδ᾽ ἐποπτεύσει θεά.

ΧΟΡΟΣ

τὸν ἄνδρ᾽ ἐκεῖνον οὔ τι μὴ λίπω ποτέ.                     225

ΑΠΟΛΛΩΝ

σὺ δ᾽ οὖν δίωκε καὶ πόνον πλείω τίθου.

ΧΟΡΟΣ

τιμὰς σὺ μὴ σύντεμνε τὰς ἐμὰς λόγῳ.

ΑΠΟΛΛΩΝ

οὐδ᾽ ἂν δεχοίμην ὥστ᾽ ἔχειν τιμὰς σέθεν.

ΧΟΡΟΣ

μέγας γὰρ ἔμπας πὰρ Διὸς θρόνοις λέγῃ.
ἐγὼ δ᾽, ἄγει γὰρ αἷμα μητρῷον, δίκας                      230
μέτειμι τόνδε φῶτα κἀκκυνηγετῶ.

APOLLO
What about a wife who kills her husband?

CHORUS LEADER
That's not blood murder in the family.

APOLLO
                                        What?
What about Zeus and his queen Hera—
your actions bring disgrace on them.
You ignore the strongest bonds between them.
Your claim dishonours Aphrodite, too,
goddess of love, from whom all men derive
their greatest joys. With man and woman
a marriage sealed by fate is stronger
than any oath, and justice guards it.
Now, if one partner kills the other one,
and you're not interested in punishment,                    [220]
if you feel no urge to act, then I say
the way you chase Orestes is unjust.
I don't see why in one case you're so harsh
when you don't really care about the other.
However, goddess Athena will take charge—
she'll organize a trial.

CHORUS LEADER
                              But that fugitive—
he'll never be free of me, never.

APOLLO
Then go after him. Bring yourself more trouble.

CHORUS LEADER
Don't try to curb my powers with your words.

APOLLO
Your powers? Those I wouldn't take,
not even as a gift.

CHORUS LEADER
                          Of course not.
You're already great, by all accounts—
right by Zeus' throne. But for my part,
since I'm called onward by a mother's blood,              [230]
I'll chase this man with justice of my own.
I scent the trail!

Aeschylus

ΑΠΟΛΛΩΝ

ἐγὼ δ' ἀρήξω τὸν ἱκέτην τε ῥύσομαι·
δεινὴ γὰρ ἐν βροτοῖσι κἀν θεοῖς πέλει
τοῦ προστροπαίου μῆνις, εἰ προδῶ σφ' ἑκών.

ΟΡΕΣΤΗΣ

ἄνασσ' Ἀθάνα, Λοξίου κελεύμασιν                    235
ἥκω, δέχου δὲ πρευμενῶς ἀλάστορα,
οὐ προστρόπαιον οὐδ' ἀφοίβαντον χέρα,
ἀλλ' ἀμβλὺς ἤδη προστετριμμένος τε πρὸς
ἄλλοισιν οἴκοις καὶ πορεύμασιν βροτῶν.
ὅμοια χέρσον καὶ θάλασσαν ἐκπερῶν,                 240
σῴζων ἐφετμὰς Λοξίου χρηστηρίους,
πρόσειμι δῶμα καὶ βρέτας τὸ σόν, θεά.
αὐτοῦ φυλάσσων ἀναμένω τέλος δίκης.

ΧΟΡΟΣ

εἶέν· τόδ' ἐστὶ τἀνδρὸς ἐκφανὲς τέκμαρ.
ἕπου δὲ μηνυτῆρος ἀφθέγκτου φραδαῖς.             245
τετραυματισμένον γὰρ ὡς κύων νεβρὸν
πρὸς αἷμα καὶ σταλαγμὸν ἐκματεύομεν.
πολλοῖς δὲ μόχθοις ἀνδροκμῆσι φυσιᾷ
σπλάγχνον· χθονὸς γὰρ πᾶς πεποίμανται τόπος,
ὑπέρ τε πόντον ἀπτέροις ποτήμασιν              250
ἦλθον διώκουσ', οὐδὲν ὑστέρα νεώς.
καὶ νῦν ὅδ' ἐνθάδ' ἐστί που καταπτακών.
ὀσμὴ βροτείων αἱμάτων με προσγελᾷ.

ὅρα ὅρα μάλ' αὖ,
λεύσσετε πάντα, μὴ                                   255
λάθῃ φύγδα βὰς
[ὁ ] ματροφόνος ἀτίτας.

22

APOLLO
I'll help my suppliant
and bring him safely home. With gods and men
the anger of a man who seeks redemption
will be dreadful, if, of my own free will,
I abandon him.

*[Apollo exits into the inner shrine. The scene now changes to Athens, just outside the Temple of Athena. Orestes enters and move up to the large statue of Athena]*

ORESTES
Queen Athena,
I've come here on Apollo's orders.
I beg your kindness. Please let me enter,
a man accursed, an outcast. I don't seek
ritual purification—my hands are clean—
but my avenging zeal has lost its edge,
worn down, blunted by other people's homes,
by all well-beaten pathways known to men.
I've stayed true to what Apollo told me
at his oracle. Crossing land and sea,                    [240]
I've reached this statue by your shrine at last.
Here I take up my position, goddess.
I await the outcome of my trial.

*[Enter the Furies, like hunting dogs, still tracking Orestes by his scent. They do not see him at first]*

CHORUS LEADER
Ah ha! Here we have that man's clear scent,
a silent witness, but firm evidence.
After him! Like hounds chasing a wounded fawn,
we track him by the drops of blood he sheds.
Man-killing work—the effort wearies me.
My lungs are bursting. We've roamed everywhere,
exploring all the regions of the earth,
crossing seas in wingless flight, moving on          [250]
faster than any ship, always in pursuit.
Now he's cornered here, cowering somewhere.
I smell human blood—I could laugh for joy!
Start looking for him! Seek him out again!
Check everywhere. Don't let him escape.
That man killed his mother—he must pay!

— ὁ δ᾽ αὖτέ γ᾽ [οὖν] ἀλκὰν ἔχων
περὶ βρέτει πλεχθεὶς θεᾶς ἀμβρότου
ὑπόδικος θέλει γενέσθαι χρεῶν.                    260

— τὸ δ᾽ οὐ πάρεστιν· αἷμα μητρῷον χαμαὶ
δυσαγκόμιστον, παπαῖ,
τὸ διερὸν πέδοι χύμενον οἴχεται.

— ἀλλ᾽ ἀντιδοῦναι δεῖ σ᾽ ἀπὸ ζῶντος ῥοφεῖν
ἐρυθρὸν ἐκ μελέων πέλανον· ἀπὸ δὲ σοῦ          265
φεροίμαν βοσκὰν πώματος δυσπότου·

— καὶ ζῶντά σ᾽ ἰσχνάνασ᾽ ἀπάξομαι κάτω,
ἀντίποιν᾽ ὡς τίνῃς ματροφόνου δύας.

— ὄψει δὲ κεἴ τις ἄλλος ἤλιτεν βροτῶν
ἢ θεὸν ἢ ξένον                                    270
τιν᾽ ἀσεβῶν ἢ τοκέας φίλους,
ἔχονθ᾽ ἕκαστον τῆς δίκης ἐπάξια.

— μέγας γὰρ Ἅιδης ἐστὶν εὔθυνος βροτῶν
ἔνερθε χθονός,
δελτογράφῳ δὲ πάντ᾽ ἐπωπᾷ φρενί.                275

ΟΡΕΣΤΗΣ
ἐγὼ διδαχθεὶς ἐν κακοῖς ἐπίσταμαι
πολλοὺς καθαρμούς, καὶ λέγειν ὅπου δίκη
σιγᾶν θ᾽ ὁμοίως· ἐν δὲ τῷδε πράγματι
φωνεῖν ἐτάχθην πρὸς σοφοῦ διδασκάλου.
βρίζει γὰρ αἷμα καὶ μαραίνεται χερός,            280
μητροκτόνον μίασμα δ᾽ ἔκπλυτον πέλει·
ποταίνιον γὰρ ὂν πρὸς ἑστίᾳ θεοῦ
Φοίβου καθαρμοῖς ἠλάθη χοιροκτόνοις.
πολὺς δέ μοι γένοιτ᾽ ἂν ἐξ ἀρχῆς λόγος,
ὅσοις προσῆλθον ἀβλαβεῖ ξυνουσίᾳ.               285

*Eumenides*

*[The Chorus of Furies catch sight of Orestes and crowd around him]*

CHORUS *[different individuals]*
— He's over there! Claiming sanctuary,
   at that statue of the eternal goddess,
   embracing it. He must want a trial,
   a judgment on his murderous violence.                      [260]

— Impossible! A mother's blood, once shed,
   soaks in the earth and can't come back again—
   the flowing stream moves through the ground,
   then disappears forever.

— No. You must pay me back.
   I'll suck your blood.
   Drinking your living bones sustains me—
   I feed upon your pain.

— Though it wears me out, I'll drag you down,
   still living, to the world below. And there
   you'll pay for murdering your mother.

— You'll see there other human criminals
   who've failed to honour gods and strangers,            [270]
   who've abused the parents they should love.
   They all receive the justice they deserve.

— Hades, mighty god of all the dead,
   judges mortal men below the ground.
   His perceptive mind records all things.

ORESTES
   My misery has been my teacher—
   I know that men are cleansed in many ways,
   that sometimes it's appropriate to speak,
   sometimes to stay silent. And in this case
   a wise master has ordered me to speak.
   Blood on my hands is dormant now, fading—            [280]
   polluting stains from my mother's murder
   have been washed away. When they were fresh,
   Apollo in his temple cleansed my guilt—
   slaughtering pigs to make me pure again.
   It's a long story to describe for you,
   right from the start, all the men I've seen,
   ones I've stayed with, then left unharmed.

25

Aeschylus

[χρόνος καθαιρεῖ πάντα γηράσκων ὁμοῦ.]
καὶ νῦν ἀφ' ἁγνοῦ στόματος εὐφήμως καλῶ
χώρας ἄνασσαν τῆσδ' Ἀθηναίαν ἐμοὶ
μολεῖν ἀρωγόν· κτήσεται δ' ἄνευ δορὸς
αὐτόν τε καὶ γῆν καὶ τὸν Ἀργεῖον λεὼν                    290
πιστὸν δικαίως ἐς τὸ πᾶν τε σύμμαχον.
ἀλλ' εἴτε χώρας ἐν τόποις Λιβυστικοῖς,
Τρίτωνος ἀμφὶ χεῦμα γενεθλίου πόρου,
τίθησιν ὀρθὸν ἢ κατηρεφῆ πόδα,
φίλοις ἀρήγουσ', εἴτε Φλεγραίαν πλάκα                    295
θρασὺς ταγοῦχος ὡς ἀνὴρ ἐπισκοπεῖ,
ἔλθοι—κλύει δὲ καὶ πρόσωθεν ὢν θεός—
ὅπως γένοιτο τῶνδ' ἐμοὶ λυτήριος.

ΧΟΡΟΣ
οὔτοι σ' Ἀπόλλων οὐδ' Ἀθηναίας σθένος
ῥύσαιτ' ἂν ὥστε μὴ οὐ παρημελημένον                     300
ἔρρειν, τὸ χαίρειν μὴ μαθόνθ' ὅπου φρενῶν,
ἀναίματον βόσκημα δαιμόνων, σκιάν.
οὐδ' ἀντιφωνεῖς, ἀλλ' ἀποπτύεις λόγους,
ἐμοὶ τραφείς τε καὶ καθιερωμένος;
καὶ ζῶν με δαίσεις οὐδὲ πρὸς βωμῷ σφαγείς·              305
ὕμνον δ' ἀκούσῃ τόνδε δέσμιον σέθεν.

— ἄγε δὴ καὶ χορὸν ἅψωμεν, ἐπεὶ
μοῦσαν στυγερὰν
ἀποφαίνεσθαι δεδόκηκεν,
λέξαι τε λάχη τὰ κατ' ἀνθρώπους                         310
ὡς ἐπινωμᾷ στάσις ἁμά.
εὐθυδίκαιοι δ' οἰόμεθ' εἶναι·
τὸν μὲν καθαρὰς χεῖρας προνέμοντ'
οὔτις ἐφέρπει μῆνις ἀφ' ἡμῶν,
ἀσινὴς δ' αἰῶνα διοιχνεῖ·                               315

26

Time destroys all things which age with time.
Now, with full reverence and holy speech,
I invoke Athena, this country's queen.
I beg her help. Let her appear unarmed.
She'll win true allies in me, my land,                      [290]
the Argive people. We'll trust her forever.
No matter where she is—in Libya,
in some region by the springs of Triton,
her birthplace, with her covered feet at rest
or on the move, assisting those she loves,
or whether, like some bold commander
in the Phlegraean plain, battle site
of gods and giants, she surveys the field—
I pray she'll come, for she's a goddess
and hears me, even though she's far away.
May she come here. May she deliver me.

CHORUS LEADER

But Apollo's power will not save you—
nor will Athena's. You're slated to die                     [300]
abandoned and alone, without a sense
of heartfelt joy, a bloodless criminal
sucked dry by demons, just a shade—no more.

[Orestes makes no answer]

What? You ignore my words and won't reply,
you, a victim fattened up for me,
my consecrated gift? You'll not perish
on any altar—no, I'll eat you alive.

[Orestes continues to remain silent]

All right then, hear our song, a spell to chain you.

CHORUS

Come, let's link our arms and dance—
Furies determined to display
our fearful art, to demonstrate
collective power we possess                                 [310]
to guide all mortals' lives.

We claim we represent true justice.
Our anger never works against
a man whose hands are clean—
all his life he stays unharmed.

27

ὅστις δ' ἀλιτὼν ὥσπερ ὅδ' ἀνὴρ
χεῖρας φονίας ἐπικρύπτει,
μάρτυρες ὀρθαὶ τοῖσι θανοῦσιν
παραγιγνόμεναι πράκτορες αἵματος
αὐτῷ τελέως ἐφάνημεν.                                    320

μᾶτερ ἅ μ' ἔτικτες, ὦ μᾶτερ
Νύξ, ἀλαοῖσι καὶ δεδορκόσιν
ποινάν, κλῦθ'. ὁ Λατοῦς γὰρ ἶ-
νίς μ' ἄτιμον τίθησιν
τόνδ' ἀφαιρούμενος                                        325
πτῶκα, ματρῷον ἅ-
γνισμα κύριον φόνου.

ἐπὶ δὲ τῷ τεθυμένῳ
τόδε μέλος, παρακοπά,
παραφορὰ φρενοδαλής,                                       330
ὕμνος ἐξ Ἐρινύων,
δέσμιος φρενῶν, ἀφόρ-
μικτος, αὐονὰ βροτοῖς.

τοῦτο γὰρ λάχος διανταία
Μοῖρ' ἐπέκλωσεν ἐμπέδως ἔχειν,                              335
θνατῶν τοῖσιν αὐτουργίαι
ξυμπέσωσιν μάταιοι,
τοῖς ὁμαρτεῖν, ὄφρ' ἂν
γᾶν ὑπέλθῃ· θανὼν δ'
οὐκ ἄγαν ἐλεύθερος.                                        340

ἐπὶ δὲ τῷ τεθυμένῳ
τόδε μέλος, παρακοπά,
παραφορὰ φρενοδαλής,

28

But those men guilty of some crime,
as this one is, who hide away,
concealing blood-stained hands—
we harass them as testament
to those they've murdered.
Blood avengers, always in pursuit,
we chase them to the end.                              [320]

Hear me, Mother Night,
mother who gave birth to me
so I could avenge
the living and the dead.
Leto's child, Apollo,
dishonours me—he tears
that man out of my hands,
the hare who cowers there,
who by rights must expiate
his mother's blood.

Let this frenzied song of ours
fall upon our victim's head,
our sacrifice—our frenzy
driving him to madness—
obliterate his mind.                                   [330]
This is our Furies' chant
It chains up the soul,
destroys its harmony,
and withers mortal men.

Remorseless Fate gave us this work
to carry on forever, a destiny
spun out for us alone,
to attach ourselves to those
who, overcome with passion,
slaughter blood relatives.
We chase after them until the end,
until they go beneath the ground.
In death they find small freedom.                      [340]

Let this frenzied song of ours
fall upon our victim's head,
our sacrifice—our frenzy
driving him to madness—
obliterate his mind.

29

ὕμνος ἐξ Ἐρινύων,
δέσμιος φρενῶν, ἀφόρ- 345
μικτος, αὐονὰ βροτοῖς.

γιγνομέναισι λάχη τάδ᾽ ἐφ᾽ ἁμὶν ἐκράνθη·
ἀθανάτων δ᾽ ἀπέχειν χέρας, οὐδέ τις ἐστί 350
συνδαίτωρ μετάκοινος·
παλλεύκων δὲ πέπλων ἀπόμοιρος ἄκληρος ἐτύχθην
‒ ⏑ ‒ ⏑ ‒ ⏑ ‒.

δωμάτων γὰρ εἰλόμαν
ἀνατροπάς, ὅταν Ἄρης 355
τιθασὸς ὢν φίλον ἕλῃ.
ἐπὶ τὸν ὧδ᾽ ἱέμεναι
κρατερὸν ὄνθ᾽ ὅμως ἀμαυ-
ροῦμεν ὑφ᾽ αἵματος νέου.

σπεύδομεν αἵδ᾽ ἀφελεῖν τινὰ τάσδε μερίμνας,
θεῶν δ᾽ ἀτέλειαν ἐμαῖς μελέταις ἐπικραίνειν,
μηδ᾽ εἰς ἄγκρισιν ἐλθεῖν·
Ζεὺς δ᾽ αἱμοσταγὲς ἀξιόμισον ἔθνος τόδε λέσχας
ἇς ἀπηξιώσατο.

<δωμάτων γὰρ εἰλόμαν
ἀνατροπάς, ὅταν Ἄρης
τιθασὸς ὢν φίλον ἕλῃ.
ἐπὶ τὸν ὧδ᾽ ἱέμεναι
κρατερὸν ὄνθ᾽ ὅμως ἀμαυ-
ροῦμεν ὑφ᾽ αἵματος νέου.>

δόξαι τ᾽ ἀνδρῶν καὶ μάλ᾽ ὑπ᾽ αἰθέρι σεμναὶ
τακόμεναι κατὰ γᾶν μινύθουσιν ἄτιμοι

30

This is our Furies' chant.
It chains up the soul,
destroys its harmony,
and withers mortal men.

These rights are ours from birth—
even the immortal gods                                    [350]
may not lay hands on us.
We share no feasts with them,
no fellowship—their pure white robes
are no part of our destiny.

The task I take upon myself is mine,
to overthrow whole families,
when strife inside the home
kills someone near and dear.
We chase that murderer down,
the one who's spilled fresh blood.
For all his strength, we wear him down.

That's why we're now here,
eager to contest the charge,
to challenge other gods,                                  [360]
to make sure none of them
ends up controlling what is ours.
There will be no trial—
for Zeus despises us,
considers us unworthy,
refusing to converse with us
because we deal in blood.

The task I take upon myself is mine,
to overthrow whole families,
when strife inside the home
kills someone near and dear.
We chase that murderer down,
the one who's spilled fresh blood.
For all his strength, we wear him down.

Those proud opinions people have,
who raise themselves so high,
who puff themselves to heaven,
will melt away, dissolving
in dishonour underground,

ἀμετέραις ἐφόδοις μελανείμοσιν, ὀρχη-     370
σμοῖς τ' ἐπιφθόνοις ποδός.

μάλα γὰρ οὖν ἁλομένα
ἀνέκαθεν βαρυπεσῆ
καταφέρω ποδὸς ἀκμάν,
σφαλερὰ ⟨καὶ⟩ τανυδρόμοις     375
κῶλα, δύσφορον ἄταν.

πίπτων δ' οὐκ οἶδεν τόδ' ὑπ' ἄφρονι λύμα·
τοῖον [γὰρ] ἐπὶ κνέφας ἀνδρὶ μύσος πεπόταται,
καὶ δνοφεράν τιν' ἀχλὺν κατὰ δώματος αὐδᾶ-
ται πολύστονος φάτις.     380

⟨μάλα γὰρ οὖν ἁλομένα
ἀνέκαθεν βαρυπεσῆ
καταφέρω ποδὸς ἀκμάν,
σφαλερὰ καὶ τανυδρόμοις
κῶλα, δύσφορον ἄταν.⟩

μένει γάρ. εὐμήχανοί
τε καὶ τέλειοι, κακῶν
τε μνήμονες σεμναὶ
καὶ δυσπαρήγοροι βροτοῖς,
ἄτιμ' ἀτίετα διόμεναι     385
λάχη θεῶν διχοστατοῦντ' ἀνηλίῳ
λάμπᾳ, δυσοδοπαίπαλα
δερκομένοισι καὶ δυσομμάτοις ὁμῶς.

τίς οὖν τάδ' οὐχ ἅζεταί
τε καὶ δέδοικεν βροτῶν,     390
ἐμοῦ κλύων θεσμὸν
τὸν μοιρόκραντον ἐκ θεῶν
δοθέντα τέλεον; ἔτι δέ μοι

when we, in our black robes,
beat out our vengeful dance—                    [370]
when we launch our attack.

Leaping from the heights,
we pound them with our feet—
our force trips up the runner
as he sprints for home,
a fate he cannot bear.

His mind is so confused
he does not sense his fall.
Dark clouds of his defilement
hover all around the man.
Murky shadows fall,
enveloping his home—
and Rumour spreads
a tale of sorrow.                               [380]

Leaping from the heights,
we pound them with our feet—
our force trips up the runner
as he sprints for home,
a fate he cannot bear.

So things remain.
We have our skills—
our powers we fulfill,
keeping human evil in our minds.
Our awesome powers
cannot be appeased by men.
Dishonoured and despised,
we see our work gets done.
Split off from gods,
with no light from the sun,
we make the path more arduous
for those who still can see
and for the blind.

What man is not in awe
or stands there unafraid                        [390]
to hear me state my rights,
those powers allowed by Fate
and ratified by all the gods,
mine to hold forever?

⟨μένει⟩ γέρας παλαιόν, οὐδ᾽ ἀτιμίας
κύρω, καίπερ ὑπὸ χθόνα                                               395
τάξιν ἔχουσα καὶ δυσήλιον κνέφας.

ΑΘΗΝΑ

πρόσωθεν ἐξήκουσα κληδόνος βοὴν
ἀπὸ Σκαμάνδρου γῆν καταφθατουμένη,
ἣν δῆτ᾽ Ἀχαιῶν ἄκτορές τε καὶ πρόμοι,
τῶν αἰχμαλώτων χρημάτων λάχος μέγα,                     400
ἔνειμαν αὐτόπρεμνον εἰς τὸ πᾶν ἐμοί,
ἐξαίρετον δώρημα Θησέως τόκοις·
ἔνθεν διώκουσ᾽ ἦλθον ἄτρυτον πόδα,
πτερῶν ἄτερ ῥοιβδοῦσα κόλπον αἰγίδος.
[πώλοις ἀκμαίοις τόνδ᾽ ἐπιζεύξασ᾽ ὄχον]                    405
καινὴν δ᾽ ὁρῶσα τήνδ᾽ ὁμιλίαν χθονὸς
ταρβῶ μὲν οὐδέν, θαῦμα δ᾽ ὄμμασιν πάρα.
τίνες ποτ᾽ ἐστέ; πᾶσι δ᾽ ἐς κοινὸν λέγω·
βρέτας τε τοὐμὸν τῷδ᾽ ἐφημένῳ ξένῳ,
ὑμᾶς θ᾽ ὁμοίας οὐδενὶ σπαρτῶν γένει,                         410
οὔτ᾽ ἐν θεαῖσι πρὸς θεῶν ὁρωμένας
οὔτ᾽ οὖν βροτείοις ἐμφερεῖς μορφώμασιν.
λέγειν δ᾽ ἄμομφον ὄντα τοὺς πέλας κακῶς
πρόσω δικαίων ἠδ᾽ ἀποστατεῖ θέμις.

ΧΟΡΟΣ

πεύσῃ τὰ πάντα συντόμως, Διὸς κόρη.                        415
ἡμεῖς γάρ ἐσμεν Νυκτὸς αἰανῆ τέκνα.
Ἀραὶ δ᾽ ἐν οἴκοις γῆς ὑπαὶ κεκλήμεθα.

ΑΘΗΝΑ

γένος μὲν οἶδα κληδόνας τ᾽ ἐπωνύμους.

ΧΟΡΟΣ

τιμάς γε μὲν δὴ τὰς ἐμὰς πεύσῃ τάχα.

Those old prerogatives
I still retain—they're mine.
I have my honour, too,
though my appointed place
is underneath the ground
in sunless darkness.

*[Enter Athena]*

ATHENA
I heard someone summon me from far away.
I was in Troy, by the Scamander's banks,
taking ownership of new property,
a gift from ruling leaders of Achaea,
a major part of what their spears had won,                    [400]
assigned to me entirely and forever,
a splendid gift for Theseus' sons.³
I've come from there at my untiring pace,
not flying on wings, but on this whirling cape,
a chariot yoked to horses in their prime.
Here I see an unfamiliar crowd,
strangers to this place, nothing I fear,
but astonishing to see. Who are you?
I'm talking to all those assembled here—
the stranger crouching there beside my statue,
and those of you like no one ever born,                       [410]
creatures no god has seen in goddesses,
in form a thing unknown to mortal men.
But to say such things about one's neighbour
who's done no wrong is far from just
and contravenes our customs.

CHORUS LEADER
                    Daughter of Zeus,
you'll find out everything—and briefly, too.
We are immortal children of the Night.
Below ground, where we have our homes,
we're called the Curses.

ATHENA
                    Now I know your race
I know what people call you.

CHORUS LEADER
                    But our powers—
these you'll quickly ascertain as well.

35

Aeschylus

ΑΘΗΝΑ
μάθοιμ᾽ ἄν, εἰ λέγοι τις ἐμφανῆ λόγον.     420

ΧΟΡΟΣ
βροτοκτονοῦντας ἐκ δόμων ἐλαύνομεν.

ΑΘΗΝΑ
καὶ τῷ κτανόντι ποῦ τὸ τέρμα τῆς φυγῆς;

ΧΟΡΟΣ
ὅπου τὸ χαίρειν μηδαμοῦ νομίζεται.

ΑΘΗΝΑ
ἦ καὶ τοιαύτας τῷδ᾽ ἐπιρροιζεῖς φυγάς;

ΧΟΡΟΣ
φονεὺς γὰρ εἶναι μητρὸς ἠξιώσατο.     425

ΑΘΗΝΑ
ἄλλαις ἀνάγκαις, ἤ τινος τρέων κότον;

ΧΟΡΟΣ
ποῦ γὰρ τοσοῦτο κέντρον ὡς μητροκτονεῖν;

ΑΘΗΝΑ
δυοῖν παρόντοιν ἥμισυς λόγου πάρα.

ΧΟΡΟΣ
ἀλλ᾽ ὅρκον οὐ δέξαιτ᾽ ἄν, οὐ δοῦναι θέλοι.

ΑΘΗΝΑ
κλύειν δίκαιος μᾶλλον ἢ πρᾶξαι θέλεις.     430

ΧΟΡΟΣ
πῶς δή; δίδαξον· τῶν σοφῶν γὰρ οὐ πένῃ.

ΑΘΗΝΑ
ὅρκοις τὰ μὴ δίκαια μὴ νικᾶν λέγω.

36

ATHENA
Those I'd like to learn. Please state them clearly.          [420]

CHORUS LEADER
We hound out of their homes all those who kill.

ATHENA
Once the killer flees, where does he finally go?

CHORUS LEADER
Where no one thinks of joy, for there is none.

ATHENA
Your screams would drive this man to such a flight?

CHORUS LEADER
Yes—he thought it right to kill his mother.

ATHENA
Why? Was he forced to do it? Did he fear
another person's anger?

CHORUS LEADER
                              Where's the urge
so strong to force a man to kill his mother?

ATHENA
There are two sides to this dispute. I've heard
only one half the argument.

CHORUS LEADER
                              What about the oath?
He won't deny he did it or accept
the guilt we charge him with.

ATHENA
                              Where do you stand?
You wish to be considered righteous,          [430]
but not to act with justice.

CHORUS LEADER
                              How? Teach me.
You clearly have a mind for subtleties.

ATHENA
I assert that no one should use oaths
to let injustice triumph.

37

ΧΟΡΟΣ

ἀλλ' ἐξέλεγχε, κρῖνε δ' εὐθεῖαν δίκην.

ἈΘΗΝΑ

ἦ κἀπ' ἐμοὶ τρέποιτ' ἂν αἰτίας τέλος;

ΧΟΡΟΣ

πῶς δ' οὔ; σέβουσαί γ' ἀξίαν κἀπ' ἀξίων.        435

ἈΘΗΝΑ

τί πρὸς τάδ' εἰπεῖν, ὦ ξέν', ἐν μέρει θέλεις;
λέξας δὲ χώραν καὶ γένος καὶ ξυμφορὰς
τὰς σάς, ἔπειτα τόνδ' ἀμυναθοῦ ψόγον·
εἴπερ πεποιθὼς τῇ δίκῃ βρέτας τόδε
ἧσαι φυλάσσων ἑστίας ἀμῆς πέλας        440
σεμνὸς προσίκτωρ ἐν τρόποις Ἰξίονος.
τούτοις ἀμείβου πᾶσιν εὐμαθές τί μοι.

ὈΡΕΣΤΗΣ

ἄνασσ' Ἀθάνα, πρῶτον ἐκ τῶν ὑστάτων
τῶν σῶν ἐπῶν μέλημ' ἀφαιρήσω μέγα.
οὐκ εἰμὶ προστρόπαιος, οὐδ' ἔχων μύσος        445
πρὸς χειρὶ τἠμῇ τὸ σὸν ἐφεζόμην βρέτας.
τεκμήριον δὲ τῶνδέ σοι λέξω μέγα.
ἄφθογγον εἶναι τὸν παλαμναῖον νόμος,
ἔστ' ἂν πρὸς ἀνδρὸς αἵματος καθαρσίου
σφαγαὶ καθαιμάξωσι νεοθήλου βοτοῦ.        450
πάλαι πρὸς ἄλλοις ταῦτ' ἀφιερώμεθα
οἴκοισι, καὶ βοτοῖσι καὶ ῥυτοῖς πόροις.
ταύτην μὲν οὕτω φροντίδ' ἐκποδὼν λέγω.
γένος δὲ τοὐμὸν ὡς ἔχει πεύσῃ τάχα.
Ἀργεῖός εἰμι, πατέρα δ' ἱστορεῖς καλῶς,        455
Ἀγαμέμνον', ἀνδρῶν ναυβατῶν ἁρμόστορα,

38

CHORUS LEADER

                       Question him.
Then make a righteous judgment.

ATHENA

                     Are you prepared
that I should be the one to do this,
to produce a final verdict?

CHORUS LEADER

                      Why not?
We respect your worth, as you do ours.

ATHENA

Stranger, do you have anything to say
by way of a response? State your country,
lineage, and circumstance. And then,
defend yourself against their accusations,
if you really trust the justice of your case,
as you sit here clinging to my statue,
a sacred suppliant beside my hearth,           [440]
doing what Ixion did so long ago.
Speak to me. Address all this directly.⁴

ORESTES

Queen Athena, your last words express
important doubts which I must first remove.
I'm not a suppliant in need of cleansing.
Nor have I fallen at your statue's feet
with my hands defiled. On these two points
I'll offer weighty proof. Our laws assert
a criminal polluted with blood guilt
will be denied all speech until he's cleansed
by someone authorized to purify
a man for murder, who sprinkles him
with suckling victim's blood. Some time ago,    [450]
in homes of other men, I underwent
such purification rites with slaughtered beasts,
at flowing streams, as well. So, as I say,
there are no grounds for your misgivings here.
As for my family, you'll know that soon enough—
I'm an Argive, son of Agamemnon.
You may well ask his story—he's the man
who put that naval force together.

Aeschylus

ξὺν ᾧ σὺ Τροίαν ἄπολιν Ἰλίου πόλιν
ἔθηκας. ἔφθιθ᾽ οὗτος οὐ καλῶς, μολὼν
εἰς οἶκον· ἀλλά νιν κελαινόφρων ἐμὴ
μήτηρ κατέκτα, ποικίλοις ἀγρεύμασιν          460
κρύψασ᾽, ἃ λουτρῶν ἐξεμαρτύρει φόνον.
κἀγὼ κατελθών, τὸν πρὸ τοῦ φεύγων χρόνον,
ἔκτεινα τὴν τεκοῦσαν, οὐκ ἀρνήσομαι,
ἀντικτόνοις ποιναῖσι φιλτάτου πατρός.
καὶ τῶνδε κοινῇ Λοξίας ἐπαίτιος,          465
ἄλγη προφωνῶν ἀντίκεντρα καρδίᾳ,
εἰ μή τι τῶνδ᾽ ἔρξαιμι τοὺς ἐπαιτίους.
σὺ δ᾽ εἰ δικαίως εἴτε μὴ κρῖνον δίκην·
πράξας γὰρ ἐν σοὶ πανταχῇ τάδ᾽ αἰνέσω.

ἈΘΗΝΑ

τὸ πρᾶγμα μεῖζον, εἴ τις οἴεται τόδε          470
βροτὸς δικάζειν· οὐδὲ μὴν ἐμοὶ θέμις
φόνου διαιρεῖν ὀξυμηνίτου δίκας·
ἄλλως τε καὶ σὺ μὲν κατηρτυκὼς ἐμοῖς
ἱκέτης προσῆλθες καθαρὸς ἀβλαβὴς δόμοις·
οὕτως δ᾽ ἄμομφον ὄντα σ᾽ αἰδοῦμαι πόλει.          475
αὗται δ᾽ ἔχουσι μοῖραν οὐκ εὐπέμπελον,
καὶ μὴ τυχοῦσαι πράγματος νικηφόρου,
χώρᾳ μεταῦθις ἰὸς ἐκ φρονημάτων
πέδοι πεσὼν ἄφερτος αἰανὴς νόσος.
τοιαῦτα μὲν τάδ᾽ ἐστίν· ἀμφότερα, μένειν          480
πέμπειν τε δυσπήμαντ᾽ ἀμηχάνως ἐμοί.
ἐπεὶ δὲ πρᾶγμα δεῦρ᾽ ἐπέσκηψεν τόδε,
φόνων δικαστὰς ὁρκίους αἱρουμένη
θεσμὸν τὸν εἰς ἅπαντ᾽ ἐγὼ θήσω χρόνον.

40

You worked with him to see that Ilion,
Troy's city, ceased to be. When he came home,
he died in a disgraceful way, butchered
by my mother, whose black heart snagged him          [460]
in devious hunting nets—these still exist,
attesting to that slaughter in his bath.
I was in exile at the time. I came back.
I killed my mother—that I don't deny—
to avenge the murder of my father,
whom I truly loved. For this murder
Apollo bears responsibility,
along with me. He urged me to it,
pointing out the cruel reprisals I would face
if I failed to act against the murderers.
Was what I did a righteous act or not?
That you must decide. I'll be satisfied,
no matter how you render judgment.

ATHENA

This is a serious matter, too complex          [470]
for any mortal man to think of judging.
It's not right even for me to adjudicate
such cases, where murder done in passion
merits passionate swift punishment.
Above all, you come here a suppliant
who's gone through all cleansing rituals,
who's pure and hence no danger to my shrine.
You thus have my respect, for in my view,
where my city is concerned, you're innocent.
But these Furies also have their function.
That's something we just cannot set aside.
So if they fail to triumph in this case,
they'll spread their poisonous resentment—
it will seep underground, infecting us,
bring perpetual disease upon our land,
something we can't bear. So stands the case.          [480]
Two options, each of them disastrous.
Allow one to remain, expel the other?
No, I see no way of resolving this.
But since the judgment now devolves on me,
I'll appoint human judges of this murder,
a tribunal bound by oath—I'll set it up

Aeschylus

ὑμεῖς δὲ μαρτύριά τε καὶ τεκμήρια                         485
καλεῖσθ', ἀρωγὰ τῆς δίκης ὁρκώματα·
κρίνασα δ' ἀστῶν τῶν ἐμῶν τὰ βέλτατα
ἥξω, διαιρεῖν τοῦτο πρᾶγμ' ἐτητύμως,
ὅρκον πορόντας μηδὲν ἔκδικον φράσειν.

ΧΟΡΟΣ
νῦν καταστροφαὶ νέων                                     490
θεσμίων, εἰ κρατή-
σει δίκα <τε> καὶ βλάβα
τοῦδε ματροκτόνου.
πάντας ἤδη τόδ' ἔργον εὐχερεί-
ᾳ συναρμόσει βροτούς·                                     495
πολλὰ δ' ἔτυμα παιδότρωτα
πάθεα προσμένει τοκεῦ-
σιν μεταῦθις ἐν χρόνῳ.

οὐδὲ γὰρ βροτοσκόπων
μαινάδων τῶνδ' ἐφέρ-                                      500
ψει κότος τις ἐργμάτων—
πάντ' ἐφήσω μόρον.
πεύσεται δ' ἄλλος ἄλλοθεν, προφωνῶν τὰ τῶν πέλας κακά,
λῆξιν ὑπόδοσίν τε μόχθων·                                 505
ἄκεά τ' οὐ βέβαια τλά-
μων [δέ τις] μάταν παρηγορεῖ.

μηδέ τις κικλῃσκέτω
ξυμφορᾷ τετυμμένος,
τοῦτ' ἔπος θροούμενος,                                    510
'ὦ δίκα,
ὦ θρόνοι τ' Ἐρινύων.'
ταῦτά τις τάχ' ἂν πατὴρ
ἢ τεκοῦσα νεοπαθὴς
οἶκτον οἰκτίσαιτ', ἐπει-                                  515
δὴ πίτνει δόμος δίκας.

ἔσθ' ὅπου τὸ δεινὸν εὖ,
καὶ φρενῶν ἐπίσκοπον
δεῖ μένειν καθήμενον.

42

to last forever. So you two parties,
summon your witnesses, set out your proofs,
with sworn evidence to back your stories.
Once I've picked the finest men in Athens,
I'll return. They'll rule fairly in this case,
bound by a sworn oath to act with justice.

*[Exit Athena]*

CHORUS

If his legal action triumphs,                                    [490]
if now this matricide prevails,
then newly set divine decrees
will overthrow all order.
Mortals will at once believe
that everything's permitted.
From now on parents can expect
repeated blows of suffering
inflicted by their children—
now and in time yet to come.

For Furies who keep watch on men
will bring no anger down                                        [500]
on human crimes—so then
we loose death everywhere,
all forms of killing known to man.
So one, seeing his neighbour's pain,
will ask another, "Where's this end?
When does our suffering diminish?"
But the poor wretch can offer nothing—
his remedies are vain, without effect.

So when a terrible disaster strikes
let no one make the old appeal,                                 [510]
"Justice, you Furies—hear me,
you powers on your thrones!"
It may well happen soon—
a father in despair, a mother
in some new catastrophe,
may scream out for pity,
now the house of justice falls.

Sometimes what's terrible can work
to bring about what's good.
Such terror needs to sit on guard,
to check the passionate heart.

43

ξυμφέρει                                    520
σωφρονεῖν ὑπὸ στένει.
τίς δὲ μηδὲν ἐν δέει
καρδίαν ⟨ἂν⟩ ἀνατρέφων
ἢ πόλις βροτός θ᾽ ὁμοί-
ως ἔτ᾽ ἂν σέβοι δίκαν;            525
μήτ᾽ ἀνάρχετον βίον
μήτε δεσποτούμενον
αἰνέσῃς.
παντὶ μέσῳ τὸ κράτος
θεὸς ὤπασεν, ἄλλ᾽                 530
ἄλλα δ᾽ ἐφορεύει.

ξύμμετρον δ᾽ ἔπος λέγω,
δυσσεβίας μὲν ὕβρις
τέκος ὡς ἐτύμως·
ἐκ δ᾽ ὑγιεί-                          535
ας φρενῶν ὁ πάμφιλος
καὶ πολύευκτος ὄλβος.

ἐς τὸ πᾶν δέ σοι λέγω,
βωμὸν αἴδεσαι Δίκας·
μηδέ νιν                             540
κέρδος ἰδὼν ἀθέῳ
ποδὶ λὰξ ἀτίσῃς·
ποινὰ γὰρ ἐπέσται.
κύριον μένει τέλος.
πρὸς τάδε τις τοκέων                545
σέβας εὖ προτίων
καὶ ξενοτί-
μους δόμων ἐπιστροφὰς
αἰδόμενός τις ἔστω.

ἑκὼν δ᾽ ἀνάγκας ἄτερ δίκαιος ὢν    550
οὐκ ἄνολβος ἔσται·
πανώλεθρος ⟨δ᾽⟩ οὔποτ᾽ ἂν γένοιτο.
τὸν ἀντίτολμον δέ φαμι παρβάταν
ἄγοντα πολλὰ παντόφυρτ᾽ ἄνευ δίκας

44

There is a benefit for men                                    [520]
to learn control through suffering.
For where is there a man or city—
both alike in this regard—
who still respects what's just
without a heart attuned to fear?

It's not right that men revere
a life without controls
or one enslaved by tyrants.
Those who practise moderation
in everything they do
acquire strength from god,                                    [530]
though he hands down
his other gifts in other ways.

Our words stress self-control,
for arrogance, we know,
is surely born from sacrilege.
From a healthy heart and mind
comes the happiness men love,
the joy they ask for in their prayers.

To sum up everything about this case,
I'll tell you this—Justice has an altar.
Give that full human reverence.
Don't trample it profanely underfoot                          [540]
because self-interest sees advantages.
Remember punishment will come—
that outcome's fixed and permanent.
So each of you, above all else,
should honour parents,
pay them the deference you owe,
respect all guests and strangers
you welcome in your home.

For happiness will never fail                                 [550]
the man who follows justice,
freely and without constraint.
He'll never be destroyed.
But the reckless man who goes too far,
who piles up riches for himself
in any way he can and disregards
all justice—I tell you this—

βιαίως ξὺν χρόνῳ καθήσειν       555
λαῖφος, ὅταν λάβῃ πόνος
θραυομένας κεραίας.

καλεῖ δ᾽ ἀκούοντας οὐδὲν ⟨ἐν⟩ μέσᾳ
δυσπαλεῖ τε δίνᾳ·
γελᾷ δὲ δαίμων ἐπ᾽ ἀνδρὶ θερμῷ,       560
τὸν οὔποτ᾽ αὐχοῦντ᾽ ἰδὼν ἀμαχάνοις
δύαις λαπαδνὸν οὐδ᾽ ὑπερθέοντ᾽ ἄκραν·
δι᾽ αἰῶνος δὲ τὸν πρὶν ὄλβον
ἔρματι προσβαλὼν δίκας
ὤλετ᾽ ἄκλαυτος, ἄϊστος.       565

ΑΘΗΝΑ

κήρυσσε, κῆρυξ, καὶ στρατὸν κατειργαθοῦ,
ἥ τ᾽ οὖν διάτορος Τυρσηνικὴ
σάλπιγξ, βροτείου πνεύματος πληρουμένη,
ὑπέρτονον γήρυμα φαινέτω στρατῷ.
πληρουμένου γὰρ τοῦδε βουλευτηρίου       570
σιγᾶν ἀρήγει καὶ μαθεῖν θεσμοὺς ἐμοὺς
πόλιν τε πᾶσαν εἰς τὸν αἰανῆ χρόνον
καὶ τούσδ᾽ ὅπως ἂν εὖ καταγνωσθῇ δίκη.

ΧΟΡΟΣ

ἄναξ Ἄπολλον, ὧν ἔχεις αὐτὸς κράτει.
τί τοῦδε σοὶ μέτεστι πράγματος λέγε.       575

ΑΠΟΛΛΩΝ

καὶ μαρτυρήσων ἦλθον—ἔστι γὰρ νόμῳ
ἱκέτης ὅδ᾽ ἀνὴρ καὶ δόμων ἐφέστιος
ἐμῶν, φόνου δὲ τοῦδ᾽ ἐγὼ καθάρσιος—
καὶ ξυνδικήσων αὐτός· αἰτίαν δ᾽ ἔχω

46

in time he'll have to strike his sail,
as storming torments break his ship,
as his yardarm shatters.

He screams for help.
But no one listens.
In the middle of the seas
he fights—but all in vain.
Whirlpools suck him down,
while heaven roars with laughter                    [560]
at the sight of this hot-tempered man
who used to boast with pride
he'd never come to grief
now helpless, panic stricken,
unable to ride out the waves.
He always lived for wealth—
now that, too, smashes on the reef,
the rock of Justice—he drowns,
unseen and unlamented.

*[The scene shifts to the Areopagus, the high court of Athens. Athena enters with a herald and ten citizens, the jury she has selected. A crowd of citizens enters with her. Orestes moves to the place where the accused stands]*

ATHENA
    Herald, blow the call for order in this court.
    Raise that Etruscan trumpet, fill your lungs,
    let these people hear an ear-piercing blast.
    As they crowd into this court of judgment          [570]
    it's better to have silence. The whole city
    can listen to my laws, which are eternal.
    So can these litigants. Then all will see
    the justice in our verdict for themselves.

*[Enter Apollo. He moves to stand behind Orestes]*

    Lord Apollo, you have your own domain.
    What's your role here? Announce that to us.

APOLLO
    I've come here as a witness. That man,
    the accused, according to our customs,
    came a suppliant to my shrine, my hearth.
    I purified him of the blood he spilled.
    As his advocate, I share the blame

Aeschylus

τῆς τοῦδε μητρὸς τοῦ φόνου. σὺ δ᾽ εἴσαγε          580
ὅπως <τ᾽> ἐπίστα τήνδε κύρωσον δίκην.

ΑΘΗΝΑ

ὑμῶν ὁ μῦθος, εἰσάγω δὲ τὴν δίκην·
ὁ γὰρ διώκων πρότερος ἐξ ἀρχῆς λέγων
γένοιτ᾽ ἂν ὀρθῶς πράγματος διδάσκαλος.

Χορος

πολλαὶ μέν ἐσμεν, λέξομεν δὲ συντόμως.          585
ἔπος δ᾽ ἀμείβου πρὸς ἔπος ἐν μέρει τιθείς
τὴν μητέρ᾽ εἰπὲ πρῶτον εἰ κατέκτονας.

ΟΡΕΣΤΗΣ

ἔκτεινα· τούτου δ᾽ οὔτις ἄρνησις πέλει.

ΧΟΡΟΣ

ἓν μὲν τόδ᾽ ἤδη τῶν τριῶν παλαισμάτων.

ΟΡΕΣΤΗΣ

οὐ κειμένῳ πω τόνδε κομπάζεις λόγον.          590

ΧΟΡΟΣ

εἰπεῖν γε μέντοι δεῖ σ᾽ ὅπως κατέκτανες.

ΟΡΕΣΤΗΣ

λέγω· ξιφουλκῷ χειρὶ πρὸς δέρην τεμών.

ΧΟΡΟΣ

πρὸς τοῦ δ᾽ ἐπείσθης καὶ τίνος βουλεύμασιν;

ΟΡΕΣΤΗΣ

τοῖς τοῦδε θεσφάτοισι· μαρτυρεῖ δέ μοι.

ΧΟΡΟΣ

ὁ μάντις ἐξηγεῖτό σοι μητροκτονεῖν;          595

ΟΡΕΣΤΗΣ

καὶ δεῦρό γ᾽ ἀεὶ τὴν τύχην οὐ μέμφομαι.

48

arising from his mother's murder.                              [580]
Start the trial. You understand procedure.
Confirm that with a just decision.

ATHENA *[addressing the Furies]*
Then I'll begin the trial. You speak up first.
The plaintiff opens our proceedings.
Tell us the facts. Begin at the beginning—
inform us clearly of the issues here.

CHORUS LEADER
There are many of us, but we'll keep
our speeches brief.

*[Turning to interrogate Orestes]*

                      Answer our questions,
as we put them one by one. First, tell us—
did you kill your mother?

ORESTES
                          Yes, I killed her.
I don't deny the fact.

CHORUS LEADER
                       We take first fall.
Three falls wins the match.

ORESTES
                      You gloat,                              [590]
but your opponent isn't pinned down yet.

CHORUS LEADER
Now you must describe the murder for us.
How did you kill her?

ORESTES
                      I'll tell you—
I drew my sword and slit her throat.

CHORUS LEADER
Who persuaded you to do this? Whose advice?

ORESTES
The orders of this god. He is my witness.

CHORUS LEADER
The prophet ordered you to kill your mother?

ORESTES
He did. And to this moment I have no regrets.

49

Aeschylus

ΧΟΡΟΣ
ἀλλ᾽ εἴ σε μάρψει ψῆφος, ἀλλ᾽ ἐρεῖς τάχα.

ΟΡΕΣΤΗΣ
πέποιθ᾽. ἀρωγὰς δ᾽ ἐκ τάφου πέμψει πατήρ.

ΧΟΡΟΣ
νεκροῖσί νυν πέπισθι μητέρα κτανών.

ΟΡΕΣΤΗΣ
δυοῖν γὰρ εἶχε προσβολὰς μιασμάτοιν.          600

ΧΟΡΟΣ
πῶς δή; δίδαξον τοὺς δικάζοντας τάδε.

ΟΡΕΣΤΗΣ
ἀνδροκτονοῦσα πατέρ᾽ ἐμὸν κατέκτανεν.

ΧΟΡΟΣ
τοιγὰρ σὺ μὲν ζῇς, ἡ δ᾽ ἐλευθέρα φόνῳ.

ΟΡΕΣΤΗΣ
τί δ᾽ οὐκ ἐκείνην ζῶσαν ἤλαυνες φυγῇ;

ΧΟΡΟΣ
οὐκ ἦν ὅμαιμος φωτὸς ὃν κατέκτανεν.          605

ΟΡΕΣΤΗΣ
ἐγὼ δὲ μητρὸς τῆς ἐμῆς ἐν αἵματι;

ΧΟΡΟΣ
πῶς γάρ σ᾽ ἔθρεψ᾽ ἂν ἐντός, ὦ μιαιφόνε,
ζώνης; ἀπεύχῃ μητρὸς αἷμα φίλτατον;

ΟΡΕΣΤΗΣ
ἤδη σὺ μαρτύρησον· ἐξηγοῦ δέ μοι,
Ἄπολλον, εἴ σφε σὺν δίκῃ κατέκτανον.          610
δρᾶσαι γὰρ ὥσπερ ἐστὶν οὐκ ἀρνούμεθα.
ἀλλ᾽ εἰ δίκαιον εἴτε μὴ τῇ σῇ φρενὶ
δοκεῖ τόδ᾽ αἷμα, κρῖνον, ὡς τούτοις φράσω.

50

**CHORUS LEADER**
But if the verdict lays its hands on you,
you'll change your story soon enough.

**ORESTES**
I'm confident. My father from his grave
will send the help I need.

**CHORUS LEADER**
So you trust the dead,
and yet you killed your mother?

**ORESTES**
I do, for she was guilty of two crimes.                    [600]

**CHORUS LEADER**
How so? Inform the judges on this point.

**ORESTES**
She killed her husband and my father.

**CHORUS LEADER**
But her death evens out the score for her.
You're still living.

**ORESTES**
When she was still alive
you didn't hound her into exile. Why?

**CHORUS LEADER**
She and her victim shared no common blood.

**ORESTES**
And my mother and me? Are we blood linked?

**CHORUS LEADER**
How else could she sustain you in her womb,
you murderer? Do you now reject
the closest bond there is, a mother's blood?

**ORESTES** *[turning to Apollo]*
You must give evidence, Apollo.                    [610]
Take the lead for me. Did I kill her justly?
For I don't deny I did the murder.
But whether that act of shedding blood
was just or not, as you perceive the facts,
you must decide, so I can tell the court.

51

Aeschylus

ἈΠΟΛΛΩΝ

λέξω πρὸς ὑμᾶς τόνδ᾽ Ἀθηναίας μέγαν
θεσμὸν δικαίως,—μάντις ὢν δ᾽ οὐ ψεύσομαι.      615
οὐπώποτ᾽ εἶπον μαντικοῖσιν ἐν θρόνοις,
οὐκ ἀνδρός, οὐ γυναικός, οὐ πόλεως πέρι,
ὃ μὴ κελεῦσαι Ζεὺς Ὀλυμπίων πατήρ.
τὸ μὲν δίκαιον τοῦθ᾽ ὅσον σθένει μαθεῖν,
βουλῇ πιφαύσκω δ᾽ ὔμμ᾽ ἐπισπέσθαι πατρός·      620
ὅρκος γὰρ οὔτι Ζηνὸς ἰσχύει πλέον.

ΧΟΡΟΣ

Ζεύς, ὡς λέγεις σύ, τόνδε χρησμὸν ὤπασε,
φράζειν Ὀρέστῃ τῷδε, τὸν πατρὸς φόνον
πράξαντα μητρὸς μηδαμοῦ τιμὰς νέμειν;

ἈΠΟΛΛΩΝ

οὐ γάρ τι ταὐτὸν ἄνδρα γενναῖον θανεῖν      625
διοσδότοις σκήπτροισι τιμαλφούμενον,
καὶ ταῦτα πρὸς γυναικός, οὔ τι θουρίοις
τόξοις ἑκηβόλοισιν, ὥστ᾽ Ἀμαζόνος,
ἀλλ᾽ ὡς ἀκούσῃ, Παλλὰς οἵ τ᾽ ἐφήμενοι
ψήφῳ διαιρεῖν τοῦδε πράγματος πέρι.      630
ἀπὸ στρατείας γάρ νιν ἠμποληκότα
†τὰ πλεῖστ᾽ ἄμεινον εὔφροσιν δεδεγμένη,
δροίτῃ περῶντι λουτρὰ κἀπὶ τέρματι
φᾶρος περεσκήνωσεν†, ἐν δ᾽ ἀτέρμονι
κόπτει πεδήσασ᾽ ἄνδρα δαιδάλῳ πέπλῳ.      635
ἀνδρὸς μὲν ὑμῖν οὗτος εἴρηται μόρος
τοῦ παντοσέμνου, τοῦ στρατηλάτου νεῶν.
ταύτην τοιαύτην εἶπον, ὡς δηχθῇ λεώς,
ὅσπερ τέτακται τήνδε κυρῶσαι δίκην.

APOLLO

    Let me address this high court of Athena.
    Tribunal members, what I have to say
    will proceed from justice. I'm a prophet.
    I cannot tell a lie. And never yet,
    when I've been seated in my oracle,
    have I said anything in prophecy
    concerning woman, man, or city state,
    that Olympian father Zeus did not command.
    Make sure you understand how powerful
    his justice is. That's why I urge you now—    [620]
    obey the will of Zeus, our father.
    No oath has greater strength than Zeus.

CHORUS LEADER

    Then, Zeus, according to your reasoning,
    told your oracle to give the order—
    Orestes must avenge his father's death,
    ignoring any rights his mother had.

APOLLO

    Yes. For these two things are not the same—
    he died a noble man, a special king
    who bears a sceptre given by the gods,
    an honoured king who dies by murder,
    and at a woman's hand, not in a fight
    where arrows fly in from a distance,
    as with the Amazons, but in a way
    which we'll describe for you, Athena,
    and those here ready to decide this case
    when you cast your votes. He'd just come home,    [630]
    returning from a long and harsh campaign,
    where in the eyes of loyal citizens
    he'd won success beyond all expectation.
    She welcomed him. Then, he took his bath.
    As he stepped out—still on the outer rim—
    she threw the cloak, his shroud, around him,
    just like a tent. She caught him in those robes,
    whose endless folds enclosed him like a net.
    Then she hacked him down. I'm telling you,
    that's how the splendid leader of the ships
    went to his death. As for that woman,
    I speak of her to rouse a sense of shame
    in those men chosen here to judge this case.

Aeschylus

ΧΟΡΟΣ
πατρὸς προτιμᾷ Ζεὺς μόρον τῷ σῷ λόγῳ·                    640
αὐτὸς δ᾽ ἔδησε πατέρα πρεσβύτην Κρόνον.
πῶς ταῦτα τούτοις οὐκ ἐναντίως λέγεις;
ὑμᾶς δ᾽ ἀκούειν ταῦτ᾽ ἐγὼ μαρτύρομαι.

ΑΠΟΛΛΩΝ
ὦ παντομισῆ κνώδαλα, στύγη θεῶν,
πέδας μὲν ἂν λύσειεν, ἔστι τοῦδ᾽ ἄκος                    645
καὶ κάρτα πολλὴ μηχανὴ λυτήριος·
ἀνδρὸς δ᾽ ἐπειδὰν αἷμ᾽ ἀνασπάσῃ κόνις
ἅπαξ θανόντος, οὔτις ἔστ᾽ ἀνάστασις.
τούτων ἐπῳδὰς οὐκ ἐποίησεν πατὴρ
οὑμός, τὰ δ᾽ ἄλλα πάντ᾽ ἄνω τε καὶ κάτω                  650
στρέφων τίθησιν οὐδὲν ἀσθμαίνων μένει.

ΧΟΡΟΣ
πῶς γὰρ τὸ φεύγειν τοῦδ᾽ ὑπερδικεῖς ὅρα·
τὸ μητρὸς αἷμ᾽ ὅμαιμον ἐκχέας πέδοι
ἔπειτ᾽ ἐν Ἄργει δώματ᾽ οἰκήσει πατρός;
ποίοισι βωμοῖς χρώμενος τοῖς δημίοις;                    655
ποία δὲ χέρνιψ φρατέρων προσδέξεται;

ΑΠΟΛΛΩΝ
καὶ τοῦτο λέξω, καὶ μάθ᾽ ὡς ὀρθῶς ἐρῶ.
οὐκ ἔστι μήτηρ ἡ κεκλημένου τέκνου
τοκεύς, τροφὸς δὲ κύματος νεοσπόρου.
τίκτει δ᾽ ὁ θρῴσκων, ἡ δ᾽ ἅπερ ξένῳ ξένη                660
ἔσωσεν ἔρνος, οἷσι μὴ βλάψῃ θεός.
τεκμήριον δὲ τοῦδέ σοι δείξω λόγου.
πατὴρ μὲν ἂν γένοιτ᾽ ἄνευ μητρός· πέλας
μάρτυς πάρεστι παῖς Ὀλυμπίου Διός,
οὐδ᾽ ἐν σκότοισι νηδύος τεθραμμένη,                      665
ἀλλ᾽ οἷον ἔρνος οὔτις ἂν τέκοι θεός.
ἐγὼ δέ, Παλλάς, τἄλλα θ᾽ ὡς ἐπίσταμαι,
τὸ σὸν πόλισμα καὶ στρατὸν τεύξω μέγαν,

54

CHORUS

    So your claim is Zeus thinks a father's death        [640]
    is more significant? But on his own
    he chained up his old father, Cronos.
    Does that not contradict what you've just said?
    I ask you judges to take note of this.

APOLLO

    You monsters—how all the gods detest you!
    Zeus has power to smash those chains apart.
    For that he has a remedy, many ways
    to set us free. But once a mortal's blood
    has drained into the dust, the man is dead.
    And then there's no return. My father Zeus
    has made no charms for that, though he can change    [650]
    all other things without a pause for breath.

CHORUS LEADER

    You plead to set him free. But think of this—
    will this man, who shed his mother's blood,
    who spilled it on the ground, return back home,
    to live in Argos in his father's house?
    Where are the public altars he can use,
    the family cleansing rites he can attend?

APOLLO

    I'll speak to that, as well. Make sure you note
    how right my answer is. That word mother—
    we give it to the one who bears the child.
    However, she's no parent, just a nurse
    to that new life embedded in her.
    The parent is the one who plants the seed,
    the father. Like a stranger for a stranger,    [660]
    she preserves the growing life, unless
    god injures it. And I can offer proof
    for what I say—a man can have a child
    without a mother. Here's our witness,
    here—Athena, child of Olympian Zeus.

*[Apollo points to Athena]*

    No dark womb nursed her—no goddess bears
    a child with ancestry like hers. Athena,
    since I know so many other things,
    I'll make your city and your people great.

55

Aeschylus

καὶ τόνδ' ἔπεμψα σῶν δόμων ἐφέστιον,
ὅπως γένοιτο πιστὸς εἰς τὸ πᾶν χρόνου            670
καὶ τόνδ' ἐπικτήσαιο σύμμαχον, θεά,
καὶ τοὺς ἔπειτα, καὶ τάδ' αἰανῶς μένοι
στέργειν τὰ πιστὰ τῶνδε τοὺς ἐπισπόρους.

ΑΘΗΝΑ
ἤδη κελεύω τούσδ' ἀπὸ γνώμης φέρειν
ψῆφον δικαίαν, ὡς ἅλις λελεγμένων;            675

ΧΟΡΟΣ
ἡμῖν μὲν ἤδη πᾶν τετόξευται βέλος.
μένω δ' ἀκοῦσαι πῶς ἀγὼν κριθήσεται.

ΑΘΗΝΑ
τί γάρ; πρὸς ὑμῶν πῶς τιθεῖσ', ἄμομφος ὦ;

ΑΠΟΛΛΩΝ
ἠκούσαθ' ὧν ἠκούσατ', ἐν δὲ καρδίᾳ
ψῆφον φέροντες ὅρκον αἰδεῖσθε, ξένοι.            680

ΑΘΗΝΑ
κλύοιτ' ἂν ἤδη θεσμόν, Ἀττικὸς λεώς,
πρώτας δίκας κρίνοντες αἵματος χυτοῦ.
ἔσται δὲ καὶ τὸ λοιπὸν Αἰγέως στρατῷ
αἰεὶ δικαστῶν τοῦτο βουλευτήριον.
πάγον δ' Ἄρειον τόνδ', Ἀμαζόνων ἕδραν            685
σκηνάς θ', ὅτ' ἦλθον Θησέως κατὰ φθόνον
στρατηλατοῦσαι, καὶ πόλιν νεόπτολιν
τήνδ' ὑψίπυργον ἀντεπύργωσαν τότε,
Ἄρει δ' ἔθυον, ἔνθεν ἔστ' ἐπώνυμος
πέτρα, πάγος τ' Ἄρειος· ἐν δὲ τῷ σέβας            690
ἀστῶν φόβος τε ξυγγενὴς τὸ μὴ ἀδικεῖν
σχήσει τό τ' ἦμαρ καὶ κατ' εὐφρόνην ὁμῶς,
αὐτῶν πολιτῶν μὴ 'πιχραινόντων νόμους

56

That's why I sent this man a suppliant
to your own shrine, so he might prove himself,
then place eternal trust in you, dear goddess,                    [670]
and you could win a new ally in him,
in his descendants, too, and thus create
an everlasting bond with his posterity.

ATHENA

Has each side said enough? Shall I now
instruct the judges to cast their votes,
acting on their judgment of what's just?

CHORUS LEADER

Though we've already shot our final arrow,
we'll stay to hear this contest to the end.

ATHENA

Why not? Now, as for you defendants,
what can I do to avoid your censure?

APOLLO

You have heard what you have heard.

*[To jurors]*
                                        My friends,
as you cast your ballots, make sure your hearts              [680]
respect that oath you made.

ATHENA

You citizens of Athens, you judges
at the first trial ever held for murder,
hear what I decree. Now and forever
this court of judges will be set up here
to serve Aegeus' people. This place,
this Mount of Ares, is where Amazons,
once marched in force, enraged at Theseus.
Here they pitched their tents. Then they built
a new city on the heights, with lofty walls
to match his own, making a sacrifice
to Ares, god of war, from whom this rock
derives its name, the Mount of Ares.                              [690]
From this hill Reverence and Terror,
two kindred rulers of my citizens,
will guarantee they don't commit injustice,
by day or night, unless the citizens
pollute the laws with evil innovations.

κακαῖς ἐπιρροαῖσι· βορβόρῳ δ' ὕδωρ
λαμπρὸν μιαίνων οὔποθ' εὑρήσεις ποτόν.     695
τὸ μήτ' ἄναρχον μήτε δεσποτούμενον
ἀστοῖς περιστέλλουσι βουλεύω σέβειν,
καὶ μὴ τὸ δεινὸν πᾶν πόλεως ἔξω βαλεῖν.
τίς γὰρ δεδοικὼς μηδὲν ἔνδικος βροτῶν;
τοιόνδε τοι ταρβοῦντες ἐνδίκως σέβας     700
ἔρυμά τε χώρας καὶ πόλεως σωτήριον
ἔχοιτ' ἄν, οἷον οὔτις ἀνθρώπων ἔχει,
οὔτ' ἐν Σκύθῃσιν οὔτε Πέλοπος ἐν τόποις.
κερδῶν ἄθικτον τοῦτο βουλευτήριον,
αἰδοῖον, ὀξύθυμον, εὑδόντων ὕπερ     705
ἐγρηγορὸς φρούρημα γῆς καθίσταμαι.
ταύτην μὲν ἐξέτειν' ἐμοῖς παραίνεσιν
ἀστοῖσιν εἰς τὸ λοιπόν· ὀρθοῦσθαι δὲ χρὴ
καὶ ψῆφον αἴρειν καὶ διαγνῶναι δίκην
αἰδουμένους τὸν ὅρκον. εἴρηται λόγος.     710

ΧΟΡΟΣ

καὶ μὴν βαρεῖαν τήνδ' ὁμιλίαν χθονὸς
ξύμβουλός εἰμι μηδαμῶς ἀτιμάσαι.

ΑΠΟΛΛΩΝ

κἄγωγε χρησμοὺς τοὺς ἐμούς τε καὶ Διὸς
ταρβεῖν κελεύω μηδ' ἀκαρπώτους κτίσαι.

ΧΟΡΟΣ

ἀλλ' αἱματηρὰ πράγματ' οὐ λαχὼν σέβεις,     715
μαντεῖα δ' οὐκέθ' ἁγνὰ μαντεύσῃ νέμων.

ΑΠΟΛΛΩΝ

ἦ καὶ πατήρ τι σφάλλεται βουλευμάτων
πρωτοκτόνοισι προστροπαῖς Ἰξίονος;

58

Once limpid waters are stained with mud,
you'll never find a drink. My people,
avoid both anarchy and tyranny.
I urge you to uphold this principle.
Show it due reverence. As for terror,
don't banish it completely from the city.
What mortal man is truly righteous
without being afraid? Those who sense the fear          [700]
revere what's right. With citizens like these
your country and your city will be safe,
stronger than anything possessed by men
in Pelops' country or in Scythia.
So here I now establish this tribunal,
incorruptible, magnificent,
swift in punishment—it stands above you,
your country's guardian as you lie asleep.
I've gone through this at length to urge you on,
my citizens, today and in the future.
But now you must get up, cast your ballots,
decide this case, while honouring your oath.          [710]
I'm finished—that's all I have to say.

*[The members of the tribunal begin to step forward and cast their votes into the urns]*

CHORUS LEADER
Watch out. Don't ever show us disrespect.
For our united power can crush your land.

APOLLO
Let me remind you—fear the oracles,
not just mine, but those of Zeus the Father.
Don't make them barren.

CHORUS LEADER *[to Apollo]*
                                      You interfere
in blood work that's not your proper business.
Your oracles remain no longer pure.

APOLLO
When the first man-killer Ixion
went a suppliant to Zeus for cleansing,
was Zeus wrong to treat him as he did?

59

Aeschylus

ΧΟΡΟΣ
λέγεις· ἐγὼ δὲ μὴ τυχοῦσα τῆς δίκης
βαρεῖα χώρᾳ τῇδ᾽ ὁμιλήσω πάλιν.　　　　　720

ἈΠΟΛΛΩΝ
ἀλλ᾽ ἔν τε τοῖς νέοισι καὶ παλαιτέροις
θεοῖς ἄτιμος εἶ σύ· νικήσω δ᾽ ἐγώ.

ΧΟΡΟΣ
τοιαῦτ᾽ ἔδρασας καὶ Φέρητος ἐν δόμοις·
Μοίρας ἔπεισας ἀφθίτους θεῖναι βροτούς.

ἈΠΟΛΛΩΝ
οὔκουν δίκαιον τὸν σέβοντ᾽ εὐεργετεῖν,　　　725
ἄλλως τε πάντως χὤτε δεόμενος τύχοι;

ΧΟΡΟΣ
σύ τοι παλαιὰς διανομὰς καταφθίσας
οἴνῳ παρηπάτησας ἀρχαίας θεάς.

ἈΠΟΛΛΩΝ
σύ τοι τάχ᾽ οὐκ ἔχουσα τῆς δίκης τέλος
ἐμῇ τὸν ἰὸν οὐδὲν ἐχθροῖσιν βαρύν.　　　730

ΧΟΡΟΣ
ἐπεὶ καθιππάζῃ με πρεσβῦτιν νέος,
δίκης γενέσθαι τῆσδ᾽ ἐπήκοος μένω,
ὡς ἀμφίβουλος οὖσα θυμοῦσθαι πόλει.

ἈΘΗΝΑ
ἐμὸν τόδ᾽ ἔργον, λοισθίαν κρῖναι δίκην.
ψῆφον δ᾽ Ὀρέστῃ τήνδ᾽ ἐγὼ προσθήσομαι.　　735
μήτηρ γὰρ οὔτις ἐστὶν ἥ μ᾽ ἐγείνατο,
τὸ δ᾽ ἄρσεν αἰνῶ πάντα, πλὴν γάμου τυχεῖν,
ἅπαντι θυμῷ, κάρτα δ᾽ εἰμὶ τοῦ πατρός.
οὕτω γυναικὸς οὐ προτιμήσω μόρον
ἄνδρα κτανούσης δωμάτων ἐπίσκοπον.　　　740
νικᾷ δ᾽ Ὀρέστης, κἂν ἰσόψηφος κριθῇ.
ἐκβάλλεθ᾽ ὡς τάχιστα τευχέων πάλους,
ὅσοις δικαστῶν τοῦτ᾽ ἐπέσταλται τέλος.

60

CHORUS LEADER

Argue all you want. But in this judgment
if I don't prevail, I'll be back again                    [720]
to bring this country to its knees.

APOLLO

Among all gods, old and new alike,
you have no honour. I will triumph here.

CHORUS LEADER

Just as you triumphed in the house of Pheres,
persuading Fate to free all men from death.⁵

APOLLO

Surely it's right to help a worshipper,
especially when his need is desperate?

CHORUS LEADER

You made those ancient goddesses, the Fates,
drunk on wine, then got them to suspend
the oldest rule of order we possess.

APOLLO

Well, you'll soon lose this case. Then you can spew
your poison and not hurt your enemies.                    [730]

CHORUS

You're young. You'd ride roughshod over me
because I'm old. I'll await the verdict,
see where this trial ends. I have my doubts
about my anger at this city.

ATHENA

It's now my task to give my final verdict.
And I award my ballot to Orestes.
No mother gave me birth—that's why
in everything but marriage I support
the man with all my heart, a true child
of my father Zeus. Thus, that woman's death
I won't consider more significant.
She killed her husband, guardian of their home.          [740]
If the votes are equal, Orestes wins.
Now, members of the jury, do your job.
Shake the ballots from the urns—and quickly.

*[The urns are emptied and the ballots counted]*

Aeschylus

ΟΡΕΣΤΗΣ
ὦ Φοῖβ᾽ Ἄπολλον, πῶς ἀγὼν κριθήσεται;

ΧΟΡΟΣ
ὦ Νὺξ μέλαινα μῆτερ, ἆρ᾽ ὁρᾷς τάδε;                        745

ΟΡΕΣΤΗΣ
νῦν ἀγχόνης μοι τέρματ᾽, ἢ φάος βλέπειν.

ΧΟΡΟΣ
ἡμῖν γὰρ ἔρρειν, ἢ πρόσω τιμὰς νέμειν.

ΑΠΟΛΛΩΝ
πεμπάζετ᾽ ὀρθῶς ἐκβολὰς ψήφων, ξένοι,
τὸ μὴ 'δικεῖν σέβοντες ἐν διαιρέσει.
γνώμης δ᾽ ἀπούσης πῆμα γίγνεται μέγα,                       750
βαλοῦσά τ᾽ οἶκον ψῆφος ὤρθωσεν μία.

ΑΘΗΝΑ
ἀνὴρ ὅδ᾽ ἐκπέφευγεν αἵματος δίκην·
ἴσον γάρ ἐστι τἀρίθμημα τῶν πάλων.

ΟΡΕΣΤΗΣ
ὦ Παλλάς, ὦ σώσασα τοὺς ἐμοὺς δόμους.                      755
γαίας πατρῴας ἐστερημένον σύ τοι
κατῴκισάς με· καί τις Ἑλλήνων ἐρεῖ,
'Ἀργεῖος ἀνὴρ αὖθις ἔν τε χρήμασιν
οἰκεῖ πατρῴοις, Παλλάδος καὶ Λοξίου
ἕκατι, καὶ τοῦ πάντα κραίνοντος τρίτου
σωτῆρος,' ὃς πατρῷον αἰδεσθεὶς μόρον                        760
σῴζει με, μητρὸς τάσδε συνδίκους ὁρῶν.
ἐγὼ δὲ χώρᾳ τῇδε καὶ τῷ σῷ στρατῷ
τὸ λοιπὸν εἰς ἅπαντα πλειστήρη χρόνον
ὁρκωμοτήσας νῦν ἄπειμι πρὸς δόμους,
μήτοι τιν᾽ ἄνδρα δεῦρο πρυμνήτην χθονὸς                     765
ἐλθόντ᾽ ἐποίσειν εὖ κεκασμένον δόρυ.
αὐτοὶ γὰρ ἡμεῖς ὄντες ἐν τάφοις τότε
τοῖς τἀμὰ παρβαίνουσι νῦν ὁρκώματα
ἀμηχάνοισι πράξομεν δυσπραξίαις,
ὁδοὺς ἀθύμους καὶ παρόρνιθας πόρους                        770
τιθέντες, ὡς αὐτοῖσι μεταμέλῃ πόνος·

62

ORESTES

O Phoebus Apollo, how did they vote?

CHORUS

O black mother Night, are you watching this?

ORESTES

Now for the result. Either I hang
or live on to see the light of day.

CHORUS

Either we're finished or our honour thrives.

APOLLO

Shake out all ballots, friends. Count them fairly.
Divide them with due care. Make no mistakes.
Errors in judgment now can mean disaster.                    [750]
A single ballot cast can save this house.

*[The ballots are shown to Athena]*

ATHENA

The numbers of the votes are equal—thus,
this man's acquitted of the murder charge.

ORESTES

O Pallas Athena, you've saved my house.
I'd lost my homeland—now you give it back,
and anyone in Greece can say, "This man
is once again an Argive, occupying
his father's property, thanks to Pallas,
thanks to Apollo, and thanks to Zeus,
third god and all-fulfilling saviour."                       [760]
Faced with these pleaders for my mother's cause,
Zeus chose to honour my father's death.
Now I'll go home. But first I make this oath
to your land and people for all time to come—
never will an Argive leader march in here
with spears arrayed against you. If he does,
in violation of this oath of mine,
from the grave we'll see his effort fails.
We'll bring him bad luck, trouble on the march,    [770]
send birds of evil omen over him.
He'll regret the pains his campaign brings him.

63

ὀρθουμένων δέ, καὶ πόλιν τὴν Παλλάδος
τιμῶσιν αἰεὶ τήνδε συμμάχῳ δορί,
αὐτοῖσιν ἡμεῖς ἐσμεν εὐμενέστεροι.
καὶ χαῖρε, καὶ σὺ καὶ πολισσοῦχος λεώς·      775
πάλαισμ᾽ ἄφυκτον τοῖς ἐναντίοις ἔχοις,
σωτήριόν τε καὶ δορὸς νικηφόρον.

ΧΟΡΟΣ
ἰὼ θεοὶ νεώτεροι, παλαιοὺς νόμους
καθιππάσασθε κἀκ χερῶν εἵλεσθέ μου.
ἐγὼ δ᾽ ἄτιμος ἁ τάλαινα βαρύκοτος      780
ἐν γᾷ τᾷδε, φεῦ,
ἰὸν ἰὸν ἀντιπενθῆ
μεθεῖσα καρδίας, σταλαγμὸν χθονὶ
ἄφορον· ἐκ δὲ τοῦ
λειχὴν ἄφυλλος, ἄτεκνος,      785
ἰὼ δίκα, πέδον ἐπισύμενος
βροτοφθόρους κηλῖδας ἐν χώρᾳ βαλεῖ.
στενάζω· τί ῥέξω;
γελῶμαι πολίταις.
δύσοισθ᾽ ἄπαθον.      790
ἰὼ μεγάλα τοὶ κόραι δυστυχεῖς
Νυκτὸς ἀτιμοπενθεῖς.

ΑΘΗΝΑ
ἐμοὶ πίθεσθε μὴ βαρυστόνως φέρειν.
οὐ γὰρ νενίκησθ᾽, ἀλλ᾽ ἰσόψηφος δίκη      795
ἐξῆλθ᾽ ἀληθῶς, οὐκ ἀτιμίᾳ σέθεν·
ἀλλ᾽ ἐκ Διὸς γὰρ λαμπρὰ μαρτύρια παρῆν,
αὐτός θ᾽ ὁ χρήσας αὐτὸς ἦν ὁ μαρτυρῶν,
ὡς ταῦτ᾽ Ὀρέστην δρῶντα μὴ βλάβας ἔχειν.
ὑμεῖς δὲ μὴ θυμοῦσθε μηδὲ τῇδε γῇ      800
βαρὺν κότον σκήψητε, μηδ᾽ ἀκαρπίαν
τεύξητ᾽, ἀφεῖσαι †δαιμόνων σταλάγματα,
βρωτῆρας αἰχμὰς σπερμάτων ἀνημέρους.
ἐγὼ γὰρ ὑμῖν πανδίκως ὑπίσχομαι
ἕδρας τε καὶ κευθμῶνας ἐνδίκου χθονὸς      805
λιπαροθρόνοισιν ἡμένας ἐπ᾽ ἐσχάραις
ἕξειν ὑπ᾽ ἀστῶν τῶνδε τιμαλφουμένας.

But all those who keep this oath, who honour
for all time Athena's city, allies
who fight on its behalf, such citizens
we'll treat with greater favour and good will.
And so farewell to you, Athena,
farewell to those who guard your city.
In struggles with your enemies, I hope
you catch them in a stranglehold, win out,
and gain the spear denoting victory.

*[Apollo and Orestes leave. The Furies move to surround Athena]*

CHORUS

You younger gods, you've wrenched our ancient laws
out of my grasp, then stamped them underfoot.
You heap on us dishonourable contempt.                    [780]
Now my anger turns against this land
I'll spread my poisons—how it's going to pay,
when I release this venom in my heart
to ease my grief. I'll saturate this ground.
It won't survive. From it disease will grow,
infecting leaves and children—that's justice.
Sterility will spread across the land,
contaminate the soil, destroy mankind.
What can I do now but scream out in pain?
The citizens make fun of us, the Furies.                  [790]
How can we put up with such indignity,
daughters of Night disgracefully abused,
dishonoured, shamed, our powers cast aside?

ATHENA

Let me persuade you not to spurn this trial.
You've not been beaten—the votes were fair,
the numbers equal, no disgrace to you.
But we received clear evidence from Zeus.
The one who spoke the oracle declared
Orestes should not suffer for his act.
So don't be vengeful, breathing anger                     [800]
on this land and drenching it with showers,
whose drops, like spears, will kill the seeds,
and blast its fruitfulness. I promise you
in all righteousness you'll have your place,
a subterranean cavern, yours by right.
Beside the hearth you'll sit on glittering thrones,
worshipped with reverence by my citizens.

ΧΟΡΟΣ
ἰὼ θεοὶ νεώτεροι, παλαιοὺς νόμους
καθιππάσασθε κἀκ χερῶν εἵλεσθέ μου.
ἐγὼ δ' ἄτιμος ἁ τάλαινα βαρύκοτος          810
ἐν γᾷ τᾷδε, φεῦ,
ἰὸν ἰὸν ἀντιπενθῆ
μεθεῖσα καρδίας, σταλαγμὸν χθονὶ
ἄφορον· ἐκ δὲ τοῦ
λειχὴν ἄφυλλος, ἄτεκνος,                    815
ἰὼ δίκα, πέδον ἐπισύμενος
βροτοφθόρους κηλῖδας ἐν χώρᾳ βαλεῖ.
στενάζω· τί ῥέξω;
γελῶμαι πολίταις·
δύσοισθ' ἄπαθον.                            820
ἰὼ μεγάλα τοι κόραι δυστυχεῖς
Νυκτὸς ἀτιμοπενθεῖς.

ΑΘΗΝΑ
οὐκ ἔστ' ἄτιμοι, μηδ' ὑπερθύμως ἄγαν
θεαὶ βροτῶν κτίσητε δύσκηλον χθόνα.        825
κἀγὼ πέποιθα Ζηνί, καὶ τί δεῖ λέγειν;
καὶ κλῇδας οἶδα δώματος μόνη θεῶν,
ἐν ᾧ κεραυνός ἐστιν ἐσφραγισμένος·
ἀλλ' οὐδὲν αὐτοῦ δεῖ· σὺ δ' εὐπιθὴς ἐμοὶ
γλώσσης ματαίας μὴ 'κβάλῃς ἔπη χθονί,      830
καρπὸν φέροντα πάντα μὴ πράσσειν καλῶς
κοίμα κελαινοῦ κύματος πικρὸν μένος
ὡς σεμνότιμος καὶ ξυνοικήτωρ ἐμοί·
πολλῆς δὲ χώρας τῆσδ' ἔτ' ἀκροθίνια
θύη πρὸ παίδων καὶ γαμηλίου τέλους         835
ἔχουσ' ἐς αἰεὶ τόνδ' ἐπαινέσεις λόγον.

ΧΟΡΟΣ
ἐμὲ παθεῖν τάδε, φεῦ,
ἐμὲ παλαιόφρονα κατά τε γᾶς οἰκεῖν,
φεῦ, ἀτίετον μύσος.
πνέω τοι μένος ἅπαντά τε κότον.            840

66

CHORUS

You younger gods, you've wrenched our ancient laws
out of my grasp, then stamped them underfoot.
You heap on us dishonourable contempt.                    [810]
Now my anger turns against this land
I'll spread my poisons—how it's going to pay,
when I release this venom in my heart
to ease my grief. I'll saturate this ground.
It won't survive. From it disease will grow,
infecting leaves and children—that's justice.
Sterility will spread across the land,
contaminate the soil, destroy mankind.
What can I do now but scream out in pain?
The citizens make fun of us, the Furies.
How can we put up with such indignity,                    [820]
daughters of Night disgracefully abused,
shamed, dishonoured, our powers cast aside?

ATHENA

But you've not lost honour—you're goddesses.
Don't let your anger lead you to excess,
to blast this land of men past remedy.
I have faith in Zeus. Why must I mention that?
Well, I'm the only god who knows the keys
to Zeus' arsenal where he keeps sealed
his lightning bolt. But there's no need for that.
Accept my argument. Don't let rash tongues             [830]
hurl threats against this land, condemning it
to sterile fruitlessness. Ease your anger.
Let your fury's black and bitter waves recede.
You can live with me, receive full honours.
The first fruits of this fertile land are yours,
forever, all those offerings for heirs,
for marriages—from now on they're yours.
With all this, you'll praise what I'm advising.

CHORUS

Such suffering for me.
My ancient wisdom
driven underground,
despised, dishonoured.
The shame, my shame.
This pure rage I breathe                                  [840]
consumes me utterly.

67

οἶ οἶ δᾶ, φεῦ.
τίς μ' ὑποδύεται, ⟨τίς⟩ ὀδύνα πλευράς;
θυμὸν ἄιε, μᾶτερ
Νύξ· ἀπὸ γάρ με τι-          845
μᾶν δαναιᾶν θεῶν
δυσπάλαμοι παρ' οὐδὲν ἦραν δόλοι.

ἈΘΗΝΑ

ὀργὰς ξυνοίσω σοι· γεραιτέρα γὰρ εἶ.
καὶ τῷ μὲν ⟨εἶ⟩ σὺ κάρτ' ἐμοῦ σοφωτέρα·
φρονεῖν δὲ κἀμοὶ Ζεὺς ἔδωκεν οὐ κακῶς.    850
ὑμεῖς δ' ἐς ἀλλόφυλον ἐλθοῦσαι χθόνα
γῆς τῆσδ' ἐρασθήσεσθε· προυννέπω τάδε.
οὑπιρρέων γὰρ τιμιώτερος χρόνος
ἔσται πολίταις τοῖσδε. καὶ σὺ τιμίαν
ἕδραν ἔχουσα πρὸς δόμοις Ἐρεχθέως    855
τεύξῃ παρ' ἀνδρῶν καὶ γυναικείων στόλων,
ὅσων παρ' ἄλλων οὔποτ' ἂν σχέθοις βροτῶν.
σὺ δ' ἐν τόποισι τοῖς ἐμοῖσι μὴ βάλῃς
μήθ' αἱματηρὰς θηγάνας, σπλάγχνων βλάβας
νέων, ἀοίνοις ἐμμανεῖς θυμώμασιν,    860
μήτ', ἐξελοῦσ' ὡς καρδίαν ἀλεκτόρων,
ἐν τοῖς ἐμοῖς ἀστοῖσιν ἱδρύσῃς Ἄρη
ἐμφύλιόν τε καὶ πρὸς ἀλλήλους θρασύν.
θυραῖος ἔστω πόλεμος, οὐ μόλις παρών,
ἐν ᾧ τις ἔσται δεινὸς εὐκλείας ἔρως·    865
ἐνοικίου δ' ὄρνιθος οὐ λέγω μάχην
τοιαῦθ' ἑλέσθαι σοι πάρεστιν ἐξ ἐμοῦ,
εὖ δρῶσαν, εὖ πάσχουσαν, εὖ τιμωμένην
χώρας μετασχεῖν τῆσδε θεοφιλεστάτης.

ΧΟΡΟΣ

ἐμὲ παθεῖν τάδε, φεῦ,    870
ἐμὲ παλαιόφρονα κατά τε γᾶς οἰκεῖν,
φεῦ, ἀτίετον μύσος.
πνέω τοι μένος ἅπαντά τε κότον.
οἶ οἶ δᾶ, φεῦ.
τίς μ' ὑποδύεται, τίς ὀδύνα πλευράς;    875

What sinks under my ribs
and pains my heart?
O Night, my mother,
the cunning of those gods,
too hard to overcome,
takes all my ancient powers,
and leaves me nothing.

ATHENA
I'll bear with your rage, for you are older,
and thus your wisdom far exceeds my own.
But Zeus gave me a fine intelligence as well.     [850]
So let me tell you this—if you leave here,
for this land you'll feel a lover's yearning.
As time goes on, my citizens will win
increasing honour, and you, on your thrones,
seated outside the house of Erechtheus,
a place of honour, will win more respect
from lines of men and women filing past
than you could find in all the world beyond.
So cast no stones for bloodshed on this land,
my realm. Do not corrupt our youthful hearts,
intoxicating them with rage, like wine,     [860]
or rip the heart out of a fighting cock
to set it in my people, giving them
a thirst for reckless internecine war.
Let them fight wars abroad, without restraint
in those men driven by a lust for fame.
I want no birds who fight their wars at home.
That's what I offer you. It's yours to take.
Do good things, receive good things in honour.
Take your place in a land the gods all love.

CHORUS
Such suffering for me—     [870]
my ancient wisdom
driven underground,
despised, dishonoured.
The shame, my shame.
This pure rage I breathe
consumes me utterly.
What sinks under my ribs
and pains my heart?

θυμὸν ἄιε, μᾶτερ
Νύξ· ἀπὸ γάρ με τι-
μᾶν δαναιᾶν θεῶν
δυσπάλαμοι παρ' οὐδὲν ἦραν δόλοι.　　　　880

ἈΘΗΝΑ
οὔτοι καμοῦμαί σοι λέγουσα τἀγαθά,
ὡς μήποτ' εἴπῃς πρὸς νεωτέρας ἐμοῦ
θεὸς παλαιὰ καὶ πολισσούχων βροτῶν
ἄτιμος ἔρρειν τοῦδ' ἀπόξενος πέδου.
ἀλλ' εἰ μὲν ἁγνόν ἐστί σοι Πειθοῦς σέβας;　　　885
γλώσσης ἐμῆς μείλιγμα καὶ θελκτήριον,
σὺ δ' οὖν μένοις ἄν· εἰ δὲ μὴ θέλεις μένειν,
οὔ τἂν δικαίως τῇδ' ἐπιρρέποις πόλει
μῆνίν τιν' ἢ κότον τιν' ἢ βλάβην στρατῷ.
ἔξεστι γάρ σοι τῆσδε γαμόρῳ χθονὸς　　　890
εἶναι δικαίως ἐς τὸ πᾶν τιμωμένῃ.

ΧΟΡΟΣ
ἄνασσ' Ἀθάνα, τίνα με φὴς ἔχειν ἕδραν;

ἈΘΗΝΑ
πάσης ἀπήμον' οἰζύος· δέχου δὲ σύ.

ΧΟΡΟΣ
καὶ δὴ δέδεγμαι· τίς δέ μοι τιμὴ μένει;

ἈΘΗΝΑ
ὡς μή τιν' οἶκον εὐθενεῖν ἄνευ σέθεν.　　　895

ΧΟΡΟΣ
σὺ τοῦτο πράξεις, ὥστε με σθένειν τόσον;

ἈΘΗΝΑ
τῷ γὰρ σέβοντι συμφορὰς ὀρθώσομεν.

ΧΟΡΟΣ
καί μοι πρόπαντος ἐγγύην θήσῃ χρόνου;

70

O Night, my mother,
the cunning of those gods,
too hard to overcome,
takes all my ancient powers,
and leaves me nothing.                                    [880]

ATHENA

I'll not tire of telling you your gifts,
so you can never lodge complaints that I,
a newer god, or men who guard this land
failed to revere such ancient goddesses
and cast you out in exile from our city.
No. But if you respect Persuasion,
holding in reverence that sacred power
whose soothing spell sits on my tongue,
then you should stay. If that's not your wish,
it would be unjust to vent your anger
on this city, injuring its people,
enraged at them from spite. It's up to you—
take your allotted portion of this land,          [890]
justly entitled to your share of honour.

CHORUS LEADER

Queen Athena, this place you say is ours,
what exactly is it?

ATHENA

                              One free of pain,
without anxieties. Why not accept?

CHORUS LEADER

If I do, what honours would I get?

ATHENA

Without you no house can thrive.

CHORUS LEADER

You'd do this? You'd grant me that much power?

ATHENA

I will. Together we'll enrich the lives
of all who worship us.

CHORUS LEADER

                              This promise you make—
you'll hold to it forever?

71

ἈΘΗΝΑ

ἔξεστι γάρ μοι μὴ λέγειν ἃ μὴ τελῶ.

ΧΟΡΟΣ

θέλξειν μ᾽ ἔοικας καὶ μεθίσταμαι κότου.  900

ἈΘΗΝΑ

τοιγὰρ κατὰ χθόν᾽ οὖσ᾽ ἐπικτήσῃ φίλους.

ΧΟΡΟΣ

τί οὖν μ᾽ ἄνωγας τῇδ᾽ ἐφυμνῆσαι χθονί;

ἈΘΗΝΑ

ὁποῖα νίκης μὴ κακῆς ἐπίσκοπα,
καὶ ταῦτα γῆθεν ἔκ τε ποντίας δρόσου
ἐξ οὐρανοῦ τε· κἀνέμων ἀήματα  905
εὐηλίως πνέοντ᾽ ἐπιστείχειν χθόνα·
καρπόν τε γαίας καὶ βοτῶν ἐπίρρυτον
ἀστοῖσιν εὐθενοῦντα μὴ κάμνειν χρόνῳ,
καὶ τῶν βροτείων σπερμάτων σωτηρίαν.
τῶν εὐσεβούντων δ᾽ ἐκφορωτέρα πέλοις.  910
στέργω γάρ, ἀνδρὸς φιτυποίμενος δίκην,
τὸ τῶν δικαίων τῶνδ᾽ ἀπένθητον γένος.
τοιαῦτα σοὔστι. τῶν ἀρειφάτων δ᾽ ἐγὼ
πρεπτῶν ἀγώνων οὐκ ἀνέξομαι τὸ μὴ οὐ
τήνδ᾽ ἀστύνικον ἐν βροτοῖς τιμᾶν πόλιν.  915

ΧΟΡΟΣ

δέξομαι Παλλάδος ξυνοικίαν,
οὐδ᾽ ἀτιμάσω πόλιν,
τὰν καὶ Ζεὺς ὁ παγκρατὴς Ἄρης τε
φρούριον θεῶν νέμει,
ῥυσίβωμον Ἑλλάνων ἄγαλμα δαιμόνων·  920
τ᾽ ἐγὼ κατεύχομαι
θεσπίσασα πρευμενῶς
ἐπισσύτους βίου τύχας ὀνησίμους
γαίας ἐξαμβρῦσαι  925
φαιδρὸν ἁλίου σέλας.

72

ATHENA
Yes. I don't say anything I don't fulfill.

CHORUS LEADER
Your magic's doing its work, it seems—          [900]
I feel my rage diminish.

ATHENA
                                   Then stay.
In this land you'll win more friends.

CHORUS LEADER
Let me speak out a blessing on the land.
Tell me what I might say.

ATHENA
                           Speak nothing
of brutal victories—only blessings
stemming from the earth, the ocean depths,
the heavens. Let gusting winds caress the land
in glorious sunlight, our herds and harvests
overflow with plenty, so they never fail
our citizens in time to come, whose seed
will last forever. Let their prosperity          [910]
match how well they worship you. I love
these righteous men, the way a gardener loves
his growing plants, this race now free of grief.
These things are yours to give. For my part,
I'll see this city wins triumphal fame
in deadly wars where men seek glory,
so all men celebrate victorious Athens.

CHORUS
Then we'll accept this home
and live here with Athena.
We'll never harm a place
which she and Ares
and all-powerful Zeus
hold as a fortress of the gods,
this glorious altar, the shield
for all the gods of Greece.          [920]
I make this prayer for Athens,
prophesying fine things for her—
bounteous happy harvests
bursting from the earth,
beneath a radiant sun.

Aeschylus

ἈΘΗΝΑ
τάδ᾿ ἐγὼ προφρόνως τοῖσδε πολίταις
πράσσω, μεγάλας καὶ δυσαρέστους
δαίμονας αὐτοῦ καταναασαμένη.
πάντα γὰρ αὗται τὰ κατ᾿ ἀνθρώπους      930
ἔλαχον διέπειν.
ὁ δὲ μὴ κύρσας βαρεῶν τούτων
οὐκ οἶδεν ὅθεν πληγαὶ βιότου.
τὰ γὰρ ἐκ προτέρων ἀπλακήματά νιν
πρὸς τάσδ᾿ ἀπάγει, σιγῶν <δ᾿> ὄλεθρος      935
καὶ μέγα φωνοῦντ᾿
ἐχθραῖς ὀργαῖς ἀμαθύνει.

ΧΟΡΟΣ
δενδροπήμων δὲ μὴ πνέοι βλάβα,
τὰν ἐμὰν χάριν λέγω·
φλογμός τ᾿ ὀμματοστερὴς φυτῶν, τὸ      940
μὴ περᾶν ὅρον τόπων,
μηδ᾿ ἄκαρπος αἰανὴς ἐφερπέτω νόσος,
μῆλά τ᾿ εὐθενοῦντα γᾶ
ξὺν διπλοῖσιν ἐμβρύοις      945
τρέφοι χρόνῳ τεταγμένῳ· γόνος <δ᾿>
πλουτόχθων ἑρμαίαν
δαιμόνων δόσιν τίοι.

ἈΘΗΝΑ
ἦ τάδ᾿ ἀκούετε, πόλεως φρούριον,
οἷ᾿ ἐπικραίνει; μέγα γὰρ δύναται      950
πότνι᾿ Ἐρινὺς παρά τ᾿ ἀθανάτοις
τοῖς θ᾿ ὑπὸ γαῖαν, περί τ᾿ ἀνθρώπων
φανερῶς τελέως διαπράσσουσιν,
τοῖς μὲν ἀοιδάς, τοῖς δ᾿ αὖ δακρύων
βίον ἀμβλωπὸν παρέχουσαι.      955

ΧΟΡΟΣ
ἀνδροκμῆτας δ᾿ ἀώρ-
ους ἀπεννέπω τύχας,

74

**ATHENA**

To all my citizens I'll act with kindness,
setting in place these goddesses among them—
powerful divinities, implacable—
whose office is to guide all mortals' lives                    [930]
in everything they do. If there's a man
who's never felt their weight, he's ignorant
of where life's blows arise. His father's crimes
drag him before these goddesses, and there,
for all his boasting, his destruction comes—
dread silent anger crushing him to dust.

**CHORUS**

Hear me speak my blessing—
let no winds destroy the trees
nor scorching desert heat move in                              [940]
to shrivel budding plants,
no festering blight kill off the fruit.
May Pan foster fertility
and make the flocks increase,
to every ewe twin lambs,
all born in season, and in Athens
may the earth be rich in treasure,
paying fine gifts to Hermes,
god of unexpected luck.

**ATHENA**

Do you hear that, you guardians of my city?
The blessings they will bring? They're powerful,
the sacred Furies, among immortal gods,                        [950]
among the dead below. With mortal men
it's clear they work their wills decisively,
for some a life of song, for others lives of tears.

**CHORUS**

I forbid those deadly accidents
which cut men down before their time.

νεανίδων τ' ἐπηράτων
ἀνδροτυχεῖς βιότους
δότε, κύρι' ἔχοντες,                                    960
θεαί τ' ὦ Μοῖραι
ματροκασιγνῆται,
δαίμονες ὀρθονόμοι,
παντὶ δόμῳ μετάκοινοι,
παντὶ χρόνῳ δ' ἐπιβριθεῖς                                965
ἐνδίκοις ὁμιλίαις,
πάντα τιμῶταται θεῶν.

ἈΘΗΝΑ
τάδε τοι χώρᾳ τἠμῇ προφρόνως
ἐπικραινομένων
γάνυμαι· στέργω δ' ὄμματα Πειθοῦς,                        970
ὅτι μοι γλῶσσαν καὶ στόμ' ἐπωπᾷ
πρὸς τάσδ' ἀγρίως ἀπανηναμένας·
ἀλλ' ἐκράτησε Ζεὺς ἀγοραῖος·
νικᾷ δ' ἀγαθῶν
ἔρις ἡμετέρα διὰ παντός.                                 975

ΧΟΡΟΣ
τὰν δ' ἄπληστον κακῶν
μήποτ' ἐν πόλει στάσιν
τᾷδ' ἐπεύχομαι βρέμειν.
μηδὲ πιοῦσα κόνις
μέλαν αἷμα πολιτᾶν                                        980
δι' ὀργὰν ποινᾶς
ἀντιφόνους ἄτας
ἁρπαλίσαι πόλεως.
χάρματα δ' ἀντιδιδοῖεν
κοινοφιλεῖ διανοίᾳ,                                       985
καὶ στυγεῖν μιᾷ φρενί·
πολλῶν γὰρ τόδ' ἐν βροτοῖς ἄκος.

ἈΘΗΝΑ
ἆρα φρονοῦσιν γλώσσης ἀγαθῆς
ὁδὸν εὑρίσκειν;
ἐκ τῶν φοβερῶν τῶνδε προσώπων                             990
μέγα κέρδος ὁρῶ τοῖσδε πολίταις·

76

And all you gods with rightful powers,
let our lovely girls all live                               [960]
to find a husband. Hear our prayers,
you sacred Fates, our sisters,
you children of the Night,
who apportion all things justly,
who have a place in every home,
whose righteous visitations
at all times carry weight, everywhere
most honoured of the gods.

ATHENA

I rejoice to hear these love-filled blessings
conferred upon this land. It pleases me        [970]
Persuasion kept watch on my tongue and lips,
when I met their fierce refusal. But Zeus,
the patron god of our assemblies,
has triumphed. Our struggle here for justice
has left us victorious forever.

CHORUS

I pray man-killing civil strife
may never roar aloud
within the city—may its dust                       [980]
not drink our citizen's dark blood,
nor passions for revenge incite
those wars which kill the state.
Let men give joy for joy,
united by their common love,
united in their enmities—
for that cures all human ills.

ATHENA

You see now how these Furies seek their way
with well intentioned words? I can predict
these terrifying faces will provide             [990]
my citizens all sorts of benefits.

τάσδε γὰρ εὔφρονας εὔφρονες αἰεὶ
μέγα τιμῶντες καὶ γῆν καὶ πόλιν
ὀρθοδίκαιον
πρέψετε πάντως διάγοντες.                                      995

ΧΟΡΟΣ
⟨χαίρετε⟩ χαίρετ᾽ ἐν αἰσιμίαισι πλούτου.
χαίρετ᾽ ἀστικὸς λεώς,
ἴκταρ ἥμενοι Διός,
παρθένου φίλας φίλοι
σωφρονοῦντες ἐν χρόνῳ.                                         1000
Παλλάδος δ᾽ ὑπὸ πτεροῖς
ὄντας ἅζεται πατήρ.

ΑΘΗΝΑ
χαίρετε χὐμεῖς· προτέραν δ᾽ ἐμὲ χρὴ
στείχειν θαλάμους ἀποδείξουσαν
πρὸς φῶς ἱερὸν τῶνδε προπομπῶν.                                1005
ἴτε καὶ σφαγίων τῶνδ᾽ ὑπὸ σεμνῶν
κατὰ γῆς σύμεναι τὸ μὲν ἀτηρὸν
χώρας κατέχειν, τὸ δὲ κερδαλέον
πέμπειν πόλεως ἐπὶ νίκῃ.
ὑμεῖς δ᾽ ἡγεῖσθε, πολισσοῦχοι                                  1010
παῖδες Κραναοῦ, ταῖσδε μετοίκοις.
εἴη δ᾽ ἀγαθῶν
ἀγαθὴ διάνοια πολίταις.

ΧΟΡΟΣ
χαίρετε, χαίρετε δ᾽ αὖθις, ἐπανδιπλάζω,
πάντες οἱ κατὰ πτόλιν,                                         1015
δαίμονές τε καὶ βροτοί,
Παλλάδος πόλιν νέμον-
τες· μετοικίαν δ᾽ ἐμὴν
εὖ σέβοντες οὔτι μέμ-
ψεσθε συμφορὰς βίου.                                           1020

ΑΘΗΝΑ
αἰνῶ τε μύθους τῶνδε τῶν κατευγμάτων
πέμψω τε φέγγει λαμπάδων σελασφόρων

78

So treat them kindly, just as they are kind.
Worship them forever. Then you'll keep
your land and city on the path of justice,
in everything you do attaining glory.

CHORUS

Rejoice, rejoice
amid the riches you deserve
rejoice, you citizens,
who dwell with Zeus,
who love that virgin girl,
Athena—and she loves you.
You manifest your wisdom                               [1000]
at the proper time, nestling
underneath Athena's wings,
while Zeus looks on in awe.

*[Enter a group citizens to lead Athena's procession, some bearing unlit torches, some robes, and some leading animals for sacrifice]*

ATHENA

And you too rejoice. I must lead the way,
show you to your rooms, by sacred torchlight
carried by your escort. Now you can go—
move with speed under the earth, and there
with sacred sacrificial blood hold down
what would destroy my land and send above
what brings prosperity, so that our city
may prove victorious. And now you citizens,
you children of Cranaus, king of this rock,          [1010]
lead our new residents for life away.
May all citizens look on with favour
at those who bring such favours to them.

CHORUS

Farewell, once more farewell,
all those who live in Athens,
gods and men, inhabitants
of Pallas' city. Pay us respect,
while we live here among you—
you'll have cause to celebrate
the fortunes of your lives.                           [1020]

ATHENA

My thanks to you for these words of blessing.
Now I'll send you down by blazing torchlight

Aeschylus

εἰς τοὺς ἔνερθε καὶ κατὰ χθονὸς τόπους

ξὺν προσπόλοισιν, αἵτε φρουροῦσιν βρέτας

τοὐμὸν δικαίως. ὄμμα γὰρ πάσης χθονὸς          1025

Θησῇδος ἐξίκοιτ᾽ ἂν εὐκλεὴς λόχος

παίδων, γυναικῶν, καὶ στόλος πρεσβυτίδων.

φοινικοβάπτοις ἐνδυτοῖς ἐσθήμασι

τιμᾶτε, καὶ τὸ φέγγος ὁρμάσθω πυρός,

ὅπως ἂν εὔφρων ἥδ᾽ ὁμιλία χθονὸς          1030

τὸ λοιπὸν εὐάνδροισι συμφοραῖς πρέπῃ.

ΠΡΟΠΟΜΠΟΙ

βᾶτε δόμῳ, μεγάλαι φιλότιμοι

Νυκτὸς παῖδες ἄπαιδες, ὑπ᾽ εὔφρονι πομπᾷ,

εὐφαμεῖτε δέ, χωρῖται,          1035

γᾶς ὑπὸ κεύθεσιν ὠγυγίοισιν,

[καὶ] τιμαῖς καὶ θυσίαις περίσεπτα τυχοῦσαι,

εὐφαμεῖτε δὲ πανδαμεί.

ἵλαοι δὲ καὶ σύμφρονες γᾷ          1040

δεῦρ᾽ ἴτε, σεμναί, ⟨ξὺν⟩ πυριδάπτῳ

λαμπάδι τερπόμεναι καθ᾽ ὁδόν.

ὀλολύξατε νῦν ἐπὶ μολπαῖς.

σπονδαὶ δ᾽ ἐς τὸ πᾶν ἐκ μετοίκων

Παλλάδος ἀστοῖς. Ζεὺς ⟨ὁ⟩ πανόπτας          1045

οὕτω Μοῖρά τε συγκατέβα.

ὀλολύξατε νῦν ἐπὶ μολπαῖς.

to your homes beneath the earth, with this escort
of those duty-bound to guard my statue.
That seems right. For the most precious part
of all the land of Theseus will come out,
a splendid throng of girls and mothers,
groups of older women.

*[From the processional company some women bearing scarlet robes move for-
ward to place the robes on the Furies. Athena speaks directly to them]*

Invest these Furies
with their special crimson robes. Honour them.
Then, move on with the torches, so this group,          [1030]
our fellow residents, can show the love
they bear this land, and for all time to come
bring our city strength and great good fortune.

*[The women dress the Furies in the scarlet robes and sing the final song of joy and
thanks, as the entire procession of Athena, Furies, and citizens moves off stage]*

THE WOMEN OF ATHENS
Move on with your loyal escort,
you mighty children of the Night,
children without children, no longer young,
yet glorious in your honours.
You citizens, nothing but blessings in your songs.

Deep in those primeval caverns
far underground, our sacrifices,
the sacred honours we bestow on you
will maintain our city's reverence.
All of you, nothing but blessings in your songs.

Come forward, sacred goddesses,          [1040]
benevolent and gracious to our land,
come forward with the flaming torches,
rejoicing as we move along our way.
Now raise triumphal cries to crown our song!

Peace now reigns forevermore
between Athena's people and their guests.
For all-seeing Zeus and Fate herself
have worked together for this ending.
Now raise triumphal cries to crown our song!

*[The entire group moves off singing and dancing]*

# NOTES

1. Pentheus, king of Thebes, tried to prevent the worship of the god Dionysus in Thebes. Dionysus drove the women of Thebes mad (including Pentheus' mother and aunts, who in an ecstatic frenzy tore him apart during their celebrations of Dionysus.

2. *Earth's central navel stone* was a marble monument at Apollo's Oracle at Delphi, believed to be the centre of the earth.

3. The phrase *Theseus' sons* is a reference to the Athenians.

4. Ixion, king of the Lapiths, was a legendary figure notorious for (among other things) murdering his father-in-law, who was also his guest. His name is often used to refer to the first mortal who committed murder.

5. In order to offer his mortal friend Admetus (son of Pheres) a fine gift, Apollo once tricked the Fates into getting drunk and then promising that Admetus would not have to die early (as the Fates had already ordained) if he could find someone to take his place.